Altoon + Porter Architects

Photographers Credits
Rick Alexander/Greg Matulionis
A+P/Martin Vanderwal
Don Dubroff
Doug Franzen
Fred Licht
Jane Lidz
Erhard Pfeiffer
Walter Smalling

Renderers Credits
Robert De Rosa/Barry Zauss
Carlos Diniz & Associates

Editorial Director USA
Pierantonio Giacoppo

Chief Editor of Collection
Maurizio Vitta

Publishing Coordinator
Franca Rottola

Graphic Design
Giampaolo Pavesi

Editing
Lisa Marie Dirks
Alison Covert
Sandra Cervantes-Caraballos
Martyn J. Anderson

Colour-separation
Litofilms Italia, Bergamo

Printing
Poligrafiche Bolis, Bergamo

First published December 1998

Copyright 1998
by l'ArcaEdizioni

All rights reserved
Printed in Italy

ISBN 88-7838-050-4

Altoon + Porter Architects
Context and Conscience

Foreword by
John Morris Dixon, FAIA

Introduction by
Ronald A. Altoon, FAIA

Texts by
Nancy Egan

l'ARCAEDIZIONI

Contents

7   Foreword *by John Morris Dixon, FAIA*
8   Context and Conscience *by Ronald A. Altoon, FAIA*
15 Works

PART I
16 *Coming To Terms: Establishing Precedents*
    PROJECTS:
18 4000 Wisconsin Avenue
22 Arden Fair
26 Lincolnwood Town Center
30 The Mall at Green Hills
34 Tower Place

PART II
38 *Breaking the Rules: An Aesthetic Evolution*
    PROJECTS:
40 Kaahumanu Center
46 Fashion Valley Center
52 The Gardens on El Paseo
56 Bighorn Institute
62 Siqueiros Mural Shade Structure
66 Echo/Horizon School
70 MCA Employee Services
76 Southwestern University School of Law
88 UCLA Wooden Center East and John Wooden Center Expansion
94 UCLA Parking Structure #3

PART III
98 *Trusting Intuition: An International Practice*
    PROJECTS:
100 Taman Anggrek Mall and Condominiums
106 Indonesian Projects Master Planning and Conceptual Design
107 Jakarta Hotel and Shopping Center
110 Capitol Center
112 Five Pillars
114 Warringah Mall
122 Buangkok and Sengkang Transit Stations
134 Dragon Tower
138 List of Works
140 Credits
142 List of Employees

Foreword
by John Morris Dixon, FAIA

Monumental institutional buildings are all well and good. They lend distinction to the localities where they are built (witness the newfound fame of Bilbao, Spain), and they enrich the lives of those who find the time and means to visit them.

But what about the settings of everyday life? Up to the time of the Industrial Revolution, the workaday fabric of city and village took care of itself very nicely, as builders reworked time-proven patterns. Architecturally, nobody could improve on the old quarters of Kyoto or Bukhara or Seville.

In the modern world, places for living, working, and shopping are too often shaped by shortsighted profit objectives and sales strategies: houses are marketed by curb appeal and appliance counts, office space by dollars per square foot, retail space by revenue projections.

Altoon + Porter Architects has applied most of its team's skills to one area of everyday life that clearly needs help, the retail environment. Retailing once enjoyed settings refined by ages of practice. Typically, small-scaled enterprises occupied repetitive modules, exemplified by the arcaded shopping streets of Renaissance Europe, the bazaars of the Middle East, or the ranks of stalls at a Shinto shrine. With industrialization came some other admirable retailing landmarks, such as the iron-framed market halls or awesome gallerias of the 19th century.

But when America began aggregating retail facilities into shopping centers, architects as a group did not rise to the challenge. While a few architects, notably Victor Gruen (1903-1980), contributed creatively to shaping the new centers, most of such work was entrusted to firms that had been churning out anonymous boxes on Main Street or the highway strip. Few shopping center developers had cultural ambitions, and the elite of the architecture profession, with few exceptions, considered the shopping center beyond help.

Meanwhile, the design of shopping environments was becoming ever more complicated and sensitive. The early "build-it-and-they-will-come" atmosphere gave way to competitive pressures. The public was noticing which malls were the most pleasant or least deadly to visit. As malls proliferated, more were built in localities where architectural appeal could be helpful in gaining permission to build. Exterior envelopes demanded more subtle response to context, and the special spaces between the selling areas demanded more distinction. An atrium now called for more than a fountain and a nondescript skylight.

Ronald Altoon and James Porter were among the first architects to realize that the shopping mall was becoming the new civic space, the one public environment most Americans would regularly experience. And it was quickly taking on the same role in other parts of the world.

As their firm of Altoon + Porter grew, it began raising questions about the retail environment. To what extent, for instance, could open-air gathering places replace or supplement enclosed ones? Could some mall roofs be fabric canopies? And this questioning attitude was transferred to the institutional clients who are now coming to the firm, raising new questions. Should a college build a library from scratch or revitalize an existing landmark? Can a university parking garage be a good neighbor without an elaborate disguise?

Clearly, the retail arena is a good training ground for the intricacies of today's architectural practice, and this firm is effectively applying what it has learned there.

Context and Conscience
by Ronald A. Altoon, FAIA

The design roots of Altoon + Porter Architects reach deep into the diverse physical and cultural landscape of Southern California. Strong childhood impressions of towering mountains, lush agricultural valleys, arid deserts, and expansive beaches, all within geographic proximity, gave the partners a startling awareness of the differences that occur in the natural environment. Through its extended communities of Hispanics, Blacks, Asians, and Caucasians living side-by-side, the region also demonstrated the rich contributions of a multitude of cultures – perhaps more convincingly than any other place on earth.

To our young eyes, the houses designed by Rudolph Schindler, Richard Neutra, Frank Lloyd Wright, and the architects of the extraordinary Case Study House program revealed a regional architecture distinctly responsive to place.[1] The strategy of using houses as research mechanisms influenced the partners of this practice such that we searched for a means to form our values in the same a priori fashion. But it would be retail architecture that would provide Altoon + Porter Architects with the vehicle for our discovery.

The design sensibility of the partners was further nourished by our formal educations. At our alma maters, the University of Southern California's School of Architecture and the University of California at Los Angeles, three values were emphasized consistently: natural order, built order and hierarchy, and craft.

- The first of these values, natural order, caused a rigorous analysis of the ways indigenous people respond to their various climatic and geographic contexts. From this came a profound reverence for land and culture, and the understanding that an architectural response must respect place rather than subjugate it to the architect's personal idiom.
- The second value, built order and hierarchy, spurred a rational system for evaluating the social interaction between people and place and extrapolating from that system to develop buildings. This approach established a strong sense of architectural discipline while providing for the coexistence between elements of subtle scale and those of heroic order.
- The third value was an appreciation of craft. Craft, while influenced by hierarchy and order and by the natural environment, focuses on the careful making of buildings, concept by concept, piece by piece, detail by detail.

There were certain forces that informed our sense of context: the natural forces (sun, wind, water, temperature, and the physical influence of geography and landscape), the dynamic forces (transportation and pedestrian access), and the cultural forces (the influence of built environments on the societies they serve). They all defined our foundation. However powerful the Southern California context was in establishing an aesthetic foundation, the experience of other environments provided a basis for comparison and appreciation.

Prior to joining the profession, the partners-to-be were involved in diverse careers. Jim Porter worked professionally as a big band musician. He brings the discipline and precision he learned as a musician to the structuring of business principles and relationships that form the framework of Altoon + Porter. Gary Dempster was focusing on engineering at an architectural firm. His tenacity for achieving accurate, technological solutions to complex issues and his sustained commitment to craft are the firm's inheritance from his experience. Carl Meyer's previous career was as an educator. Our concept of mentorship is the result of the nurturing values of a teacher that Carl brought to our practice.

During the same period, I did graduate studies in the studio of Louis I. Kahn at the University of Pennsylvania. It was a time when the architectural faculty included the talented academicians Robert Geddes, Ian McHarg, Robert LeRicolais, and G. Holmes Perkins. The impact of study with Kahn and McHarg fostered a lasting commitment to their principles. Kahn's incessant search for institutional order, coupled with McHarg's profound respect for ecological balance, strengthened my aesthetic foundation. In my role as the firm's design partner, I find that legacy continues to inspire our work.

Our project experiences on the East Coast made lasting impressions on each of us and affected our national perspective. Life and options in the Northeast are constrained by the effects of four seasons and by a somewhat parochial social structure. By comparison, Southern California offers a hospitable climate and an open, socially mobile society. Los Angeles is a place where *ideas* are currency, valued commodities indeed when applied in a holistic and responsible way. The disparity between these two places forced us to recognize the malleability and rich potential of the West Coast – the perfect environment for an innovative, new firm.

Los Angeles was an accommodating place to establish our identity. Here we were able to create an interactive model for a collaborative practice, one in which each partner has specific responsibilities yet every project has the benefit of all the partners' talents. This model, rooted in this place, has allowed us to meld our personal and professional backgrounds and perspectives to create an aesthetic that continues to evolve as we take our practice around the globe.

Location determined, the next step was to grow the firm from our philosophic roots. With few exceptions, well-known architects have earned initial recognition working with residential projects. It is rare for an architect specializing in hospitals, prisons, or retail work to find related work published or discussed among his peers. While less of a step-child, work in historic preservation receives little commendation.

One Pritzker Prize winner was cautioned by the pundits in the profession to give up retail commissions if he intended to be acknowledged as a worthy designer. With the prevalence of this notion in the profession, it is not surprising that many great architects test their ideas in smaller residential projects and later apply them, as mature concepts, in their institutional projects. Clearly this was the case with Meier, Gehry, Mies van der Rohe, and Kahn.

For Altoon + Porter Architects, there were no houses. Instead, we began and sustained the practice with a distinctive commercial retail portfolio. The retail arena served as the laboratory for ideas that eventually found their way into our institutional, historic, and mixed-use projects. At the same time, our approach to this building type, our constant push to refine the elements, and our cultural sensitivity has helped us to transform the retail center into a civic institution.

The challenge inherent in this transformation is not obvious. Consider the design process in an institutional building, a museum for example. From the beginning, the durability and quality of the project is understood as an imperative. The client's goals and those of the architect converge. The opportunity and circumstances are in place for the design of an extraordinary institutional building, a work of art.

When an architect undertakes a retail commission, however, the scenario is very different. There are often competing agendas: development, finance, leasing, property management, operations, security, promotions, public relations, project management, and construction. Anchor tenants – department stores who have the right to review the planning, design, and materials chosen by the architect – have their input. In addition, there are an average of 175 tenants, each of whom engage their own designers to affirm their unique identity in the project. While the quality of a museum cannot be judged by one exhibit, a retail project is often judged by store designs which are not a part of the building architect's brief. Individual storefront expression is encouraged, yet it can have a damaging effect on the coherence of the project. And then there is the time frame, which is dictated by the market. In order to create a building of the same quality as an institutional project, the commercial architect must satisfy the sometimes discordant clients as well as the marketplace, all within the strict parameters of real time and hard costs.

Managing, even subverting, the process such that the building supersedes the expectation of the building type and creates worthy architecture, represents a vastly different challenge than that posed by the museum. In the late 1970s, working together in another firm, the partners began a deliberate evolution. We transformed the dark, dreary, unordered, and nearly accidental regional shopping centers of the '60s into the bright, disciplined, institutional malls of the '80s. Piece by piece, building by building, centers that had been regarded as non-architecture metamorphosed into sophisticated examples of civic architecture. Just as the historic gallerias of Europe created a public place in cities great and small, so the retail buildings in America found a level of civic dignity.

At Altoon + Porter, we have reinvented the retail prototype to achieve a level of quality rare in this kind of building. Our success in that area encouraged us to take the lessons learned in the development of retail and mixed-use centers outside the commercial typology and give new expression to a wide range of institutional projects.

Some of that work is illustrated here. It is used to demonstrate the establishment of our foundation and the continual evolution of an aesthetic as it influenced other aspects of our practice. The work in this monograph includes institutional, historic, residential, research, and mixed-use architectural projects, as well as interior architecture.

As a background to the projects included here, we believe it is important to understand how we create. We define ourselves as one architect in four bodies. Each of the four partners holds "last word" responsibility for an area of the practice. The work of each of the partners is reviewed by the specialist partner. The firm is structured as a matrix, so that each partner contributes his expertise to every project.

James F. Porter, AIA, is Partner for Administration, controlling financial, accounting, legal, insurance, real estate, and contracts. Carl F. Meyer, AIA, is Partner for Management Services, responsible for an efficient and effective delivery process and for computer-aided design services. Gary K. Dempster, AIA, is Partner for Technical Services, overseeing construction documents, the bidding process, and construction administration. And as Partner for Design, I am responsible for establishing concepts and editing designs for planning, urban design, architecture, interior architecture, and graphic design.

Our portfolio reflects a culture of interdependence. Because of our collective contextual and philosophic roots, our work is inspired by interaction and the commitment of our talented and dedicated staff, whose efforts contributed to the works in this monograph. We also thank our clients. Without a shared vision and their willingness to consider new ideas, these projects would not have been possible.

Ronald A. Altoon, FAIA

[1] Predominantly sponsored by Art & Architecture Magazine, the Case Study Houses were commissioned as prototypes of modern architecture: well-designed, affordably-priced residences which used the most recent advances in building techniques and materials.

Altoon+Porter's Los Angeles office 1990 to the present.

Altoon+Porter's Los Angeles office December 1984 to 1990, Studio passage.

Altoon+Porter's Los Angeles office December 1984 to 1990, Library.

Works

Altoon+Porter's Los Angeles office 1990 to present, Board room.

I. Coming To Terms: Establishing Precedents

The American regional shopping center was invented in the mid-1960s. Lacking a true architectural precedent, the initial examples of the building type were, quite literally, the planning diagrams rendered in concrete and steel. However, by the mid-1980s, the retail development boom was at its height and competition was intense. Developers recognized that simply building the typical center, regardless of the quality of the location or the anchor stores, would not necessarily spell success. No longer would "facelift" renovations keep the older retail properties competitive.

The search for a competitive advantage led a number of the country's top developers to the young firm of Altoon + Porter Architects. Early in their careers, Ronald Altoon and James Porter had earned their reputations by finding creative responses that met developers' financial concerns. Their fledgling practice was beginning to gain recognition for innovation in commercial design. During the second half of the '80s, Altoon + Porter created a series of benchmark retail projects – new construction and renovations in urban and suburban environments – for some of the leading U.S. retail developers.

Part of the success of the young firm in creating distinctive projects was the partners' recognition that retail architecture had a rich history in the galleries and passages of Europe. What Altoon + Porter accomplished for its clients was to recapture the civic role of retail by giving these properties a public face of institutional quality. Not only did these projects meet the developers' needs for a highly competitive retail product that could be designed and built within budget constraints, but they satisfied the community desire for a quality shopping environment that was more than a generic box.

These retail centers also provided Altoon + Porter with fertile sites on which to nurture the firm's design aesthetic. From their formal foundation with its deep roots in context and order, the architects developed a rich vocabulary of elements and detail, a profound respect for tradition and craft, and an equal appreciation of urban and natural environs. These projects redefined retail architecture and defined Altoon + Porter Architects as a talented team well worth watching.

4000 Wisconsin Avenue

The invitation to design the firm's first significant new building presented what was to become a familiar conundrum for Altoon + Porter Architects. The developer wanted a project equal in quality to the corporate headquarters next door, but on a speculative development budget. The neighbor was a meticulously detailed Georgian Revival building that reflected the architectural legacy of the nation's capital. As a portion of the new building would be leased to the major tenant of the existing building, the design had to be sympathetic to the established architectural heritage.

Since the project is located on Wisconsin Avenue, the major urban artery connecting Georgetown and Washington D.C. with the suburb of Chevy Chase, Altoon + Porter addressed context and precedent with a strongly urban building scaled to the neighborhood. Wisconsin Avenue boasts a rich mix of residential homes, office buildings, retail shops, and notable structures including the Naval Observatory and the National Cathedral. In preparation, the architects studied the designs of historic, large-scale, public buildings in Williamsburg and Baltimore, as well as in nearby Georgetown and Alexandria. As a result, the details are adapted from classical Georgian elements, while the brick and pre-cast materials are reflective of the locale.

Perhaps the greatest challenge was to design a building layout and system that met zoning and height restrictions (a 65-foot height limitation in the District of Columbia) yet maintained the elegant façade proportion of historic buildings. The building design uses a 30-foot grid with 10-foot-6-inch, floor-to-floor heights to get the desired number of floors, but uses a special post-tension structural system that enhances office layout possibilities. On the exterior, the masonry is crafted such that the brick gives way to windows, and as the windows rise, the mass is lightened and the building climbs vertically. Corners are chiseled to reduce the overall massiveness of the structure and pre-cast concrete serves as lintels and keystones to articulate the façade.

The complex is planned as a courtyard building with the office wings defining a single central space. To the east, along Wisconsin Avenue, a motor court receives the street much like at the many embassies and chancelleries of Washington D.C. On doing this, the building links contextually to the institutional streetscape of the capital city while it connects physically and stylistically with its immediate neighbor.

As the debut commission for Altoon + Porter Architects, 4000 Wisconsin Avenue provided a rich opportunity to define the ground rules for the design aesthetic of the practice. By using traditional elements more as caricature than replica of historic buildings, the design preserves the integrity of the architectural expression rather than the structure itself. Early lessons about context were reinforced in a successful mix of uses.

View of loggia.

Façade detail.

Walkway.

Arden Fair

When Altoon + Porter Architects received the call for the renovation and expansion of Arden Fair in the late 1980s, the 1957 center needed much more than an update, it needed total redefinition. The site, located in California's capital city, allowed the firm to explore the civic role of the regional mall while reshaping this early example.

Arden Fair's renovation and expansion represented an opportunity to develop design elements that responded to the symbolism inherent in Sacramento's public institutions and to the qualities of dignity and permanence that buildings give their communities. Moreover, Arden Fair, as an independent regional center, required a strong sense of order, discipline, and clarity. The center needed to become more sophisticated to keep pace with the city's dynamic growth.

The new, civic presence at Arden Fair was achieved by the use of elements of subtle scale assembled in a heroic order. The clean vocabulary of elements – the handrail, balconies, light fixtures, paving, artwork, elevators, stairs, and escalators – work both as individual objects and as part of the large scheme. As an example, design elements from the Beaux-Arts period traditionally used for city landmarks, public monuments, and grand meeting places were modified and incorporated into the design. Also borrowed from this tradition is an 85-foot, glass-canopied rotunda that gives definition and order to the center. Outside, the skylight and roof structure are the most dramatic features, creating a position of prominence against the skyline.

The rotunda's volume of space allows for a play of light to be projected through large geometric panels suspended from the trusses. The mall's bridge structure brings the architecture overhead into an interactive position with the pedestrian zone below. The volume also allows an important unification of the east and west arcades. These arcades are topped by approximately 40,000 square feet of glass-barrel vaulting that tempers the massiveness of the building by suggesting the delicate proportions of a Victorian conservatory. Careful manipulation of natural and artificial light, combined with suspended geometric forms, gives the skylight an almost weightless position.

Arden Fair marked the beginning of a series of award-winning designs for Altoon + Porter Architects. Focusing on the use of appropriate, individual elements to create a cohesive whole, the redesign for Arden Fair matured the concept of the regional mall and gave the firm a sense of what retail architecture could be to a city and its community.

24

The arcade.   *Section diagram.*

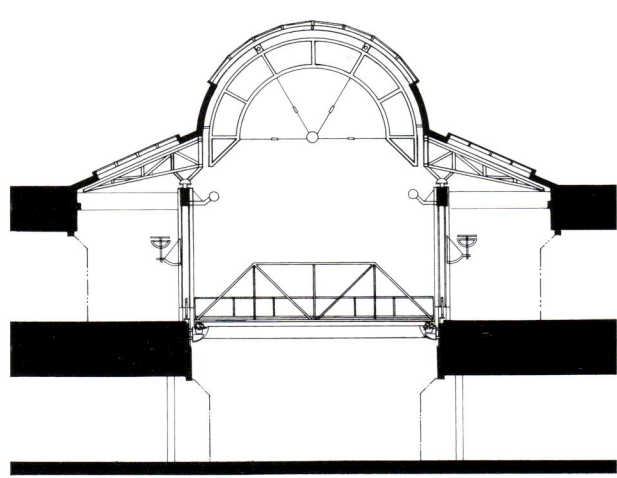

Light ring.

Integration of public art.

Lincolnwood Town Center

As you head out of Chicago's city limits, one of the first suburban communities you come to is Lincolnwood. Given the big city's strong territorial imperative, this affluent, self-contained town lacked a physical structure that would create a sense of community identity.

Lincolnwood had no true village center, nothing but strip-oriented retail. But when a 1.2-million-square-foot mall and office complex was originally proposed for the site, it was rejected by Lincolnwood officials. The development plans were seen as too large for the community. Although town leaders wanted a neighborhood center, they turned down any plan that might overpower the intimate scale that made Lincolnwood unique. Could the town have a civic structure that would be welcoming? Altoon + Porter answered that question affirmatively with Lincolnwood Town Center.

Designed to serve in one of the most hostile climates in North America, Lincolnwood Town Center is a shelter against the weather yet functions more as an urban retreat than a bastion against the cold. Optimistic, even playful in spirit, Lincolnwood is a constructivist design. In keeping with the need for a simply-scaled building, the modern, bi-level center reveals its order systematically, as if assembled from a kit of parts.

In order to emphasize this idea, the architects employed simple forms with elegant and stable materials such as brick, granite, and marble. The rugged brick and concrete exterior is offset by the use of canopies; a welcoming porte-cochère is crowned by a sloped, metal-seamed roof.

In contrast, the interior is light, airy, and quite feminine. A high, gabled roof is covered by a sparkling skylight and supplemented by smaller skylights above a second-level walkway. Together, these skylights create a distinctive atrium. Additional lighting is provided by adjustable fixtures attached to the building's frame. These decorative lights and incandescent spotlights enhance the skylight at night.

An octagonal-shaped center court was designed to house a glass observation elevator, a twin set of escalators, a raised fountain, and landscaped gardens and resting areas. Reflective of the building's straightforward approach, the interior is designed with straight aisles and clear sight lines. Large areas of glass allow shoppers to see nearly all tenants from the center court.

Lincolnwood provided Altoon + Porter the opportunity to refine its vocabulary of elements and details. The result is a civic center whose straightforward manner does not stray from its Midwestern heritage. The frequent use of the center court for public functions confirms the community's strong acceptance of the project.

Connection details.

Center court.

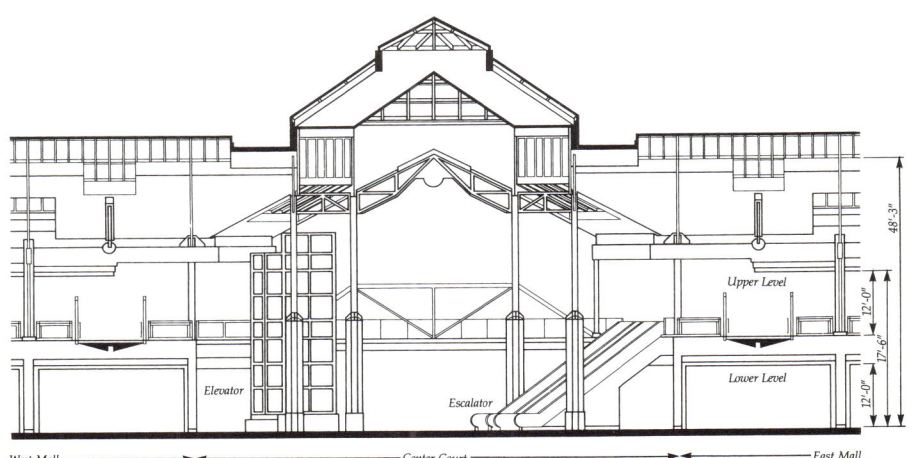

Section diagram.

The Mall at Green Hills

When Altoon + Porter Architects was commissioned to combine a free-standing department store, an open-air retail strip, and two single-level malls, the architects understood that their work was not just to connect the disparate parts, but to connect this center to the traditions of the community. Located in Nashville, Tennessee, The Mall at Green Hills reflects the old-world manners of southern gentility while adding modern vibrancy to the city. From the conglomeration of buildings, the architects created a homogenous, fully-enclosed shopping center that responds to the context of Nashville both physically and culturally.

Altoon + Porter designed the exterior of The Mall at Green Hills to correspond to the surrounding countryside, using the environment as inspiration. Deep red, native brick mimics the red earth of the land, and the forest green trim of the doors, windows, and skylight mullions recalls the architecture of the adjacent community. The architectural forms are respectful of the entry canopies and skylights that remained in place from the old structure. But Altoon + Porter clearly brought a higher institutional quality to the complex; the mall now conveys an image of permanence to the community.

In contrast with the brick exterior, the architects created a white interior space that is clean and elegant. Theatrical cornices, specialty lighting, signage, and the materials palette were all carefully chosen to establish local and historic references. The altered ambiance attracted prominent merchants and appealed to the desired customers.

The site posed several challenges, however. The addition of 130,000 square feet of shops, the unification of the mall, the integration of parking structures, and the establishment of a second level directly over an operating center all had to be completed without any extra land available for expansion. Altoon + Porter met these challenges, the result being a beautiful new mall that takes its design cues from the physical and cultural features of the South.

The Mall at Green Hills has attained the highest competitive sales in Nashville since it opened as a joined structure. Its metamorphosis from an obsolete hodgepodge of stores to a successful, contemporary shopping center has given the community an added boost in reputation and revenues and has endeared locals to the project.

Mall walkway bridge.

Lighting detail.

Details of grand court skylight.

Grand court skylight.

Details of grand court skylight.

Tower Place

The Tower Place urban infill development was part of an effort to bolster Cincinnati's battle against suburban shopping centers with the hope that an upscale retail complex would lure customers back downtown. When the developers commissioned Altoon + Porter Architects, the charge was not only to create a successful urban center, but to give the city a cultural asset as well.

In Cincinnati, Altoon + Porter found a typical, American city with a traditional architectural heritage protected by a strong urban design review board. The mandate was for a new building to compliment its neighbors in a respectful manner while establishing a distinct identity for itself. On the prominent 40,000-square-foot corner site, the architects created a formal, urban retail complex that has become a landmark, a part of the city's fabric.

Envisioned as a multi-story, urban atrium patterned after an agate, Tower Place has three levels of retail shops. The complex is hollow at the middle to transport light from 134 feet above. The retail space surrounds an enclosed glass atrium and skylight beneath which is a restaurant and sculpture fountain. At street level, the shops facing the sidewalk reinforce pedestrian interaction and shopping along the main street.

Extending the streetscape, the facility joins the landmark Carew Tower, which is on the same block, to the Omni Netherlands Hotel. On the interior, each of the three levels at Tower Place connects to the concourse, arcade, and promenade of Carew Tower. In addition to the design of the new retail at Tower Place, Altoon + Porter Architects also redefined Carew Tower's retail arcade.

Reinterpreting the diverse façades of its neighbors, the exterior skin of Tower Place was designed in limestone and pre-cast concrete and combines three distinct elements. The base allows both physical and visual access from the street and contributes to the continuity of the already established urban pattern. The middle portion shields the parking structure from view. The top cornice and roof line terminate the building, consistent with neighboring buildings.

Above the retail levels are five levels of parking, providing space for 500 vehicles. An adjacent 1,200-space structure feeds directly into the second level of retail stores via a pedestrian bridge outfitted with specialty shops. In its entirety, the complex consists of a 52-story office building, a 29-story hotel, a three-level retail center, and a garage.

In the late 1980s, Tower Place became an integral component of Cincinnati's development boom that especially affected the downtown area. Altoon + Porter's design respectfully embraces the community's values while attracting visitors and providing an invaluable asset to the city.

Above, details of the façade and its integration in the urban context. Left, the atrium skylight. Opposite page, the atrium.

37

Altoon+Porter's Los Angeles office December 1984 to 1990, Entry and reception area.

II. Breaking the Rules: An Aesthetic Evolution

A visit to an architectural office reveals a great deal about the culture and maturity of the firm. Decisions about the design and location of the office are driven by the development of the aesthetic of the practice; those decisions then change the design culture of the firm.

The partners' decision to lease space in a building with a historic sensibility – with arches and alcoves reminiscent of early California architecture – served them well as they created their first portfolio. Altoon + Porter's early work spoke of an accountability to context in a literal yet creative way. Building on their formalist foundation, the partners developed a vocabulary and a grammar, a set of rules for transforming mundane commercial projects into buildings of institutional quality and civic character.

By the time Altoon + Porter Architects had been in practice for five years, they had earned a reputation for producing commercial projects of exceptional quality. When earthquake damage induced a move to new space, the firm made a radical departure by leasing offices in an unembellished, commercial complex and then proceeded to separate the office from the simplicity of the building with a bold interior design. Was the new-found self-confidence evidenced in the design a result of the move or the cause of it? What is clear is that work produced in this open, somewhat irreverent space represents a break with the firm's own tradition. Altoon + Porter Architects had internalized a set of rules well enough to break them.

Both in diversity of project type and in response, the next phase of development for the firm reveals a willingness to push the aesthetic envelope. Whereas the earlier solutions created a new design vocabulary for commercial projects, especially retail, in the next phase, projects derive their response from a heightened sense of the contextual environment. Designed for true institutional projects or for institutional quality, commercial projects take source metaphors and architectural order, break them apart, and recompose them as projects that are at once part of their environment and distinctive icons.

40

Kaahumanu Center

In expanding a regional shopping center, Altoon + Porter Architects had the opportunity to create a new image for an existing facility. Built in 1972, the Kaahumanu Center had become a social hub with retail stores, restaurants, and theaters catering to both natives and tourists. The client wanted to increase retail and parking space while turning the center into an architectural landmark with a contemporary identity appropriate to the tropical resort environment. The architects' design captured the special flavor of Maui and its breathtaking natural features on a site where the shimmering sea, open skies, and distant mountains form a brilliant backdrop.

At the beginning of the project, the architects faced a major challenge – a processing plant and cannery for Maui Land & Pineapple Company (one of the project's owners) was located directly behind the center, restricting the planned expansion. Altoon + Porter solved the problem by suggesting the dismantling of the plant and building a new, modern facility on the opposite side of the property. This eased the horizontal and vertical expansion of the center by providing an enlarged site, and, combined with the construction of a second floor, doubled the retail capacity. Parking was also expanded around the entire facility to assure easy access.

The client desired a covered structure that would be open to the island's natural features. The designers maximized the idea of the open-air environment and combined it with a striking architectural concept that was derived from Maui's unique heritage. An undulating canopy, the most impressive feature of the new center, spans a 90-foot-by-206-foot skylight and alludes to the billowing sails of tall ships that first brought trade to the island. Its form also recalls the high clouds and distant mountains which are visible from the second floor.

The design solution is a technical masterpiece that brings the airy climate into the interior spaces. Created from multiple layers of Teflon-coated fiberglass, the roof structure is held together by tension wires. Kona winds from the mountains and trade winds from the sea circulate through the layers of the roof and are drawn inside. The skylight allows 70 percent of natural, ambient light to penetrate the interior, creating a pleasant environment during the day and night. Because the roof design uses natural ventilation, energy is conserved and operations expenses were drastically reduced. The roof structure dissipates heat buildup, prevents the need for artificial lighting during the daytime, and shields the interior spaces from the sun's ultraviolet rays. The layers also divert rain, preventing any disturbance to shopping activity.

The center was named after Queen Kaahumanu and the architects created a successful environmental graphics program based on the legacy of this beloved nineteenth-century monarch. The project's logo is an image of the queen in regal profile adorned with a wedding lei. Other architectural details were inspired by the spectacular surroundings and the native culture. Paving patterns were influenced by the play of light on the ocean's surface, coral reefs, and grass floor mats. Local flora is reflected in the handrails and carried throughout the signage program for the building directories and destination areas. Custom-designed light fixtures evoke the magic of the torch lights from island villages and are illuminated for evening activities. And exterior landscape elements and interior plantings celebrate the island's indigenous vegetation.

Main entrance portal.

Central court skylight.

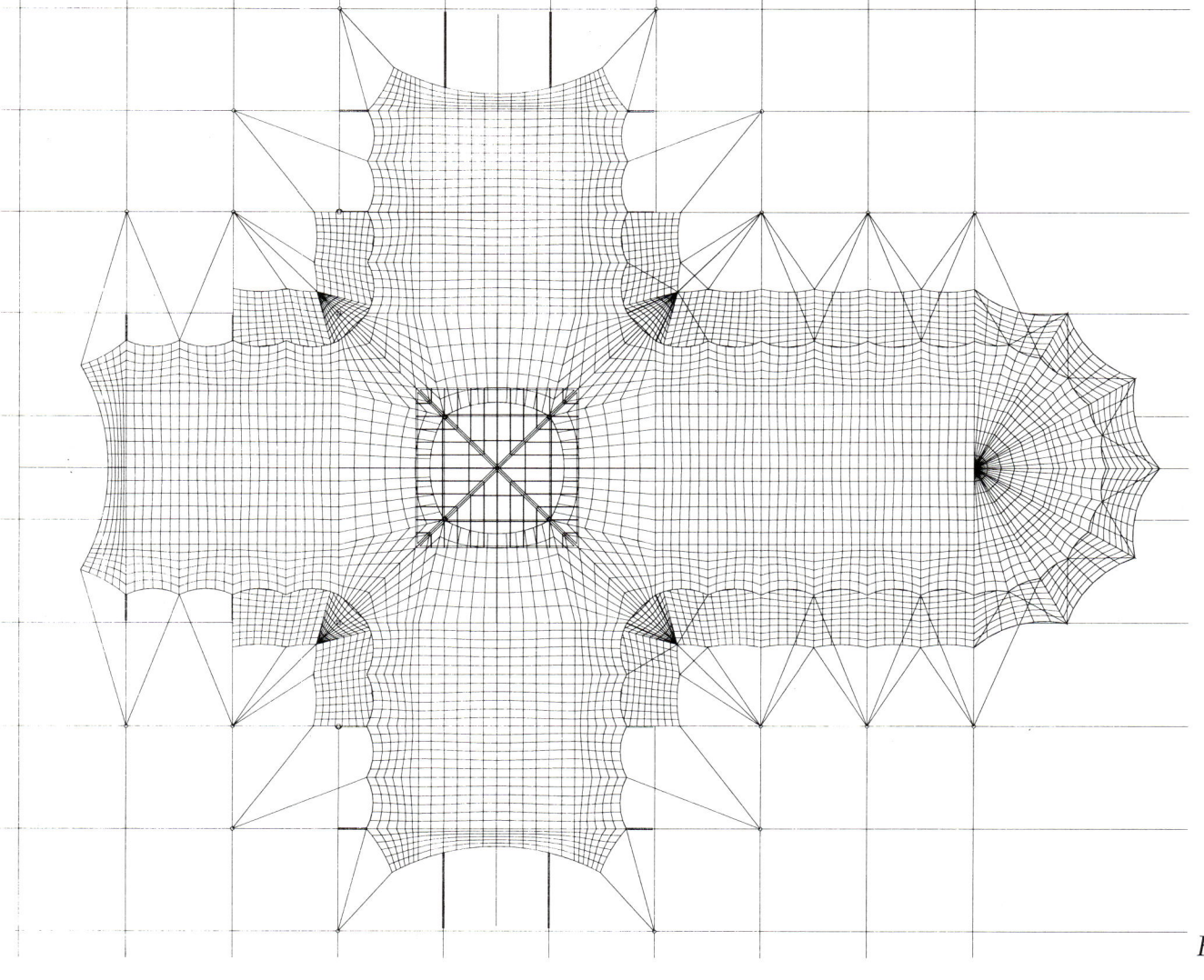

Fabric roof diagram.

44

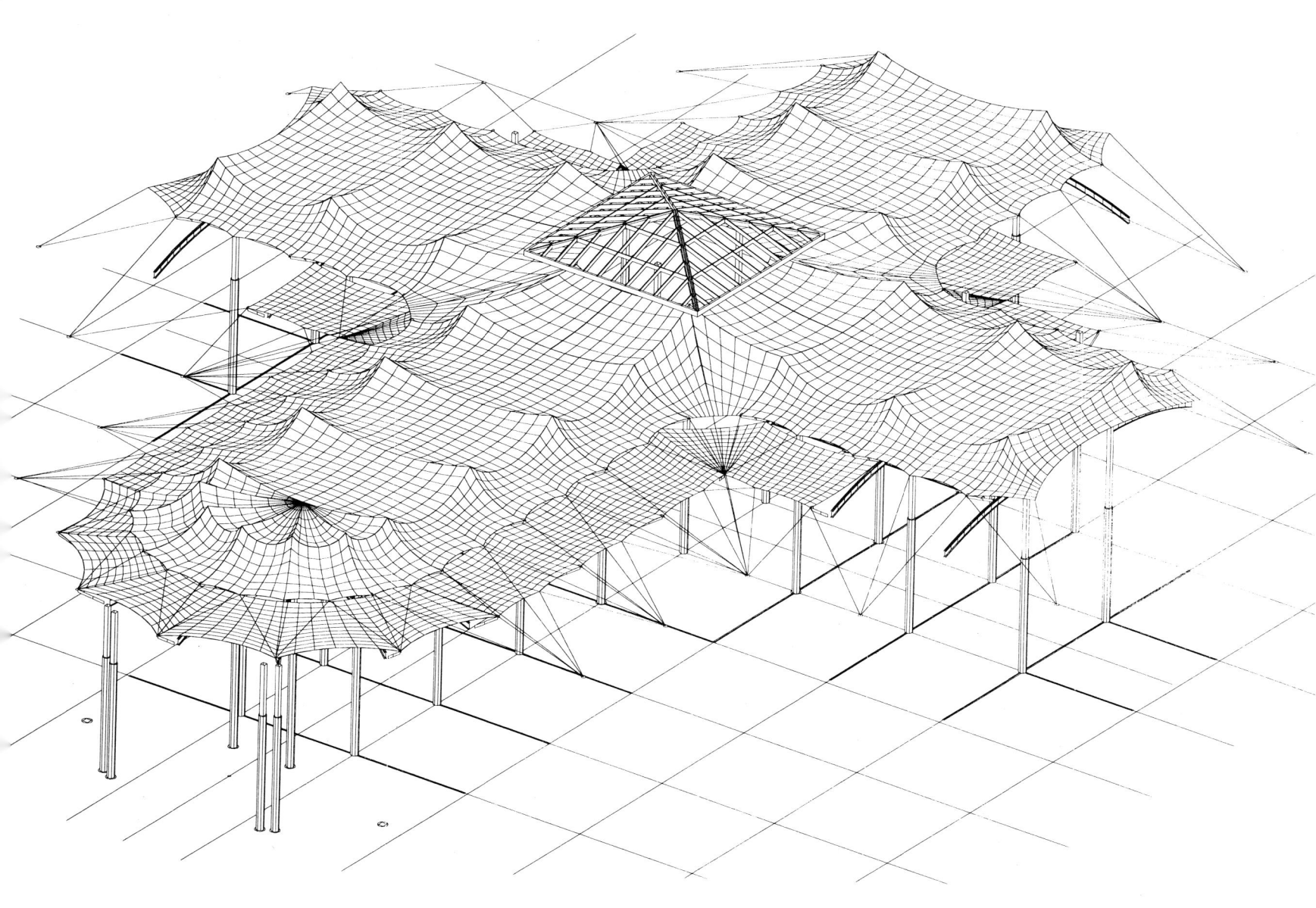

Fabric roof structure diagrams.

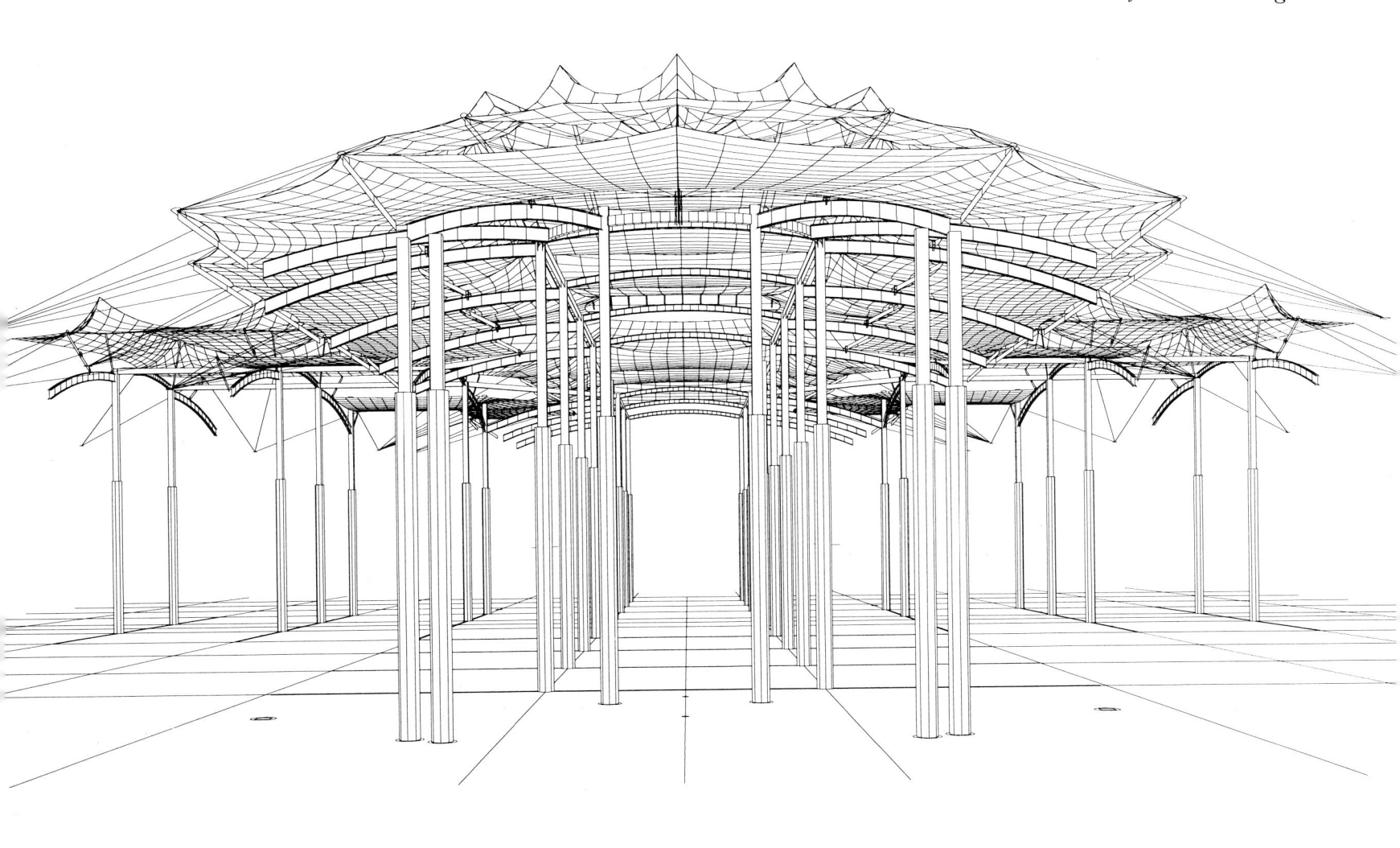

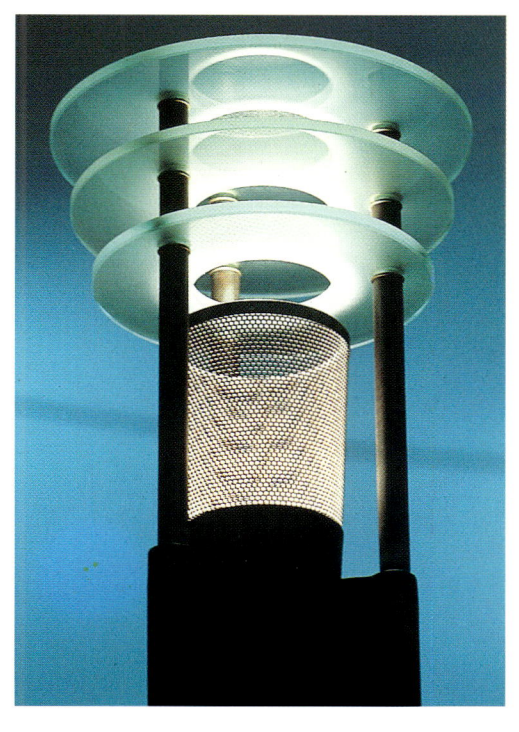

Above left, axial view of mall. Above, light fixture detail.

Left and below, details of the main entrance portal.

46

Fashion Valley Center

For many San Diego shoppers, "the mall" was Fashion Valley Center. The regional center had enjoyed popular success since it opened as a single-level, outdoor shopping experience in the late 1960s. By the mid-90s, the owners wanted to capitalize on their aging asset with a renovation and expansion program. Altoon + Porter Architects was commissioned to create a new identity for Fashion Valley that would appeal to the upscale and international tourist markets and attract more sophisticated merchants.

Repositioning at this scale – 1.7 million square feet – was no small task. The architects expanded the center vertically and connected the project to a series of new, structured parking buildings and a new light rail/bus terminal. All of this was achieved while keeping the existing merchants in business during the construction.

In spite of the size, the owners did not want a retail monolith. If they were going to attract the right market, Fashion Valley would have to be a special environment. Altoon + Porter responded with a "garden cityscape" concept that captures the essence of San Diego. Through a series of linking forms and expansion spaces, the architects created a lively outdoor environment where garden buildings grow within a city structure and city buildings are in bold juxtaposition to garden buildings.

Using the existing center's simple, linear design as a background, Altoon + Porter changed the image of the mall with an architecture of bold, abstract forms that define individual shopping precincts. Prominent, formal city structures punctuate the casual open garden spaces to create nodes of identity. This sense of zone is multiplied several times throughout the project to give the visitor numerous experiences and choices as they move through the center. The connective tissue that allows the continuous interplay of the formal and casual across the project is a collection of trellises, awnings, and canopies. Materials that recall San Diego's architectural heritage – stone, plaster, ceramic tile, and ornamental metal – also serve to integrate the precincts into the overall project.

What was once a suburban site is now part of the heavily trafficked, urban fabric of greater San Diego. Constrained on the north and south by parking structures and bounded by the river, transit station, and trolley lines on the south, the center needed a visible urban face but found little room for it. Altoon + Porter overcame the site restriction with the creation of three major arrival gates that use distinctive architectural elements to establish the new image for the familiar center.

With shops, restaurants, terrace dining, a food court, and a multi-screen cinema, shoppers experience the Fashion Valley's garden cityscape as an alternative to traditional urban space where they meet to shop, to dine, to watch a film, or just to socialize. The transformation of Fashion Valley Center, currently the largest redesigned mall in the United States, sets a benchmark in the design of the new, retail/entertainment prototype. Altoon + Porter's use of the retail precincts defined by striking abstractions of "city-garden" architecture has changed the shape of shopping.

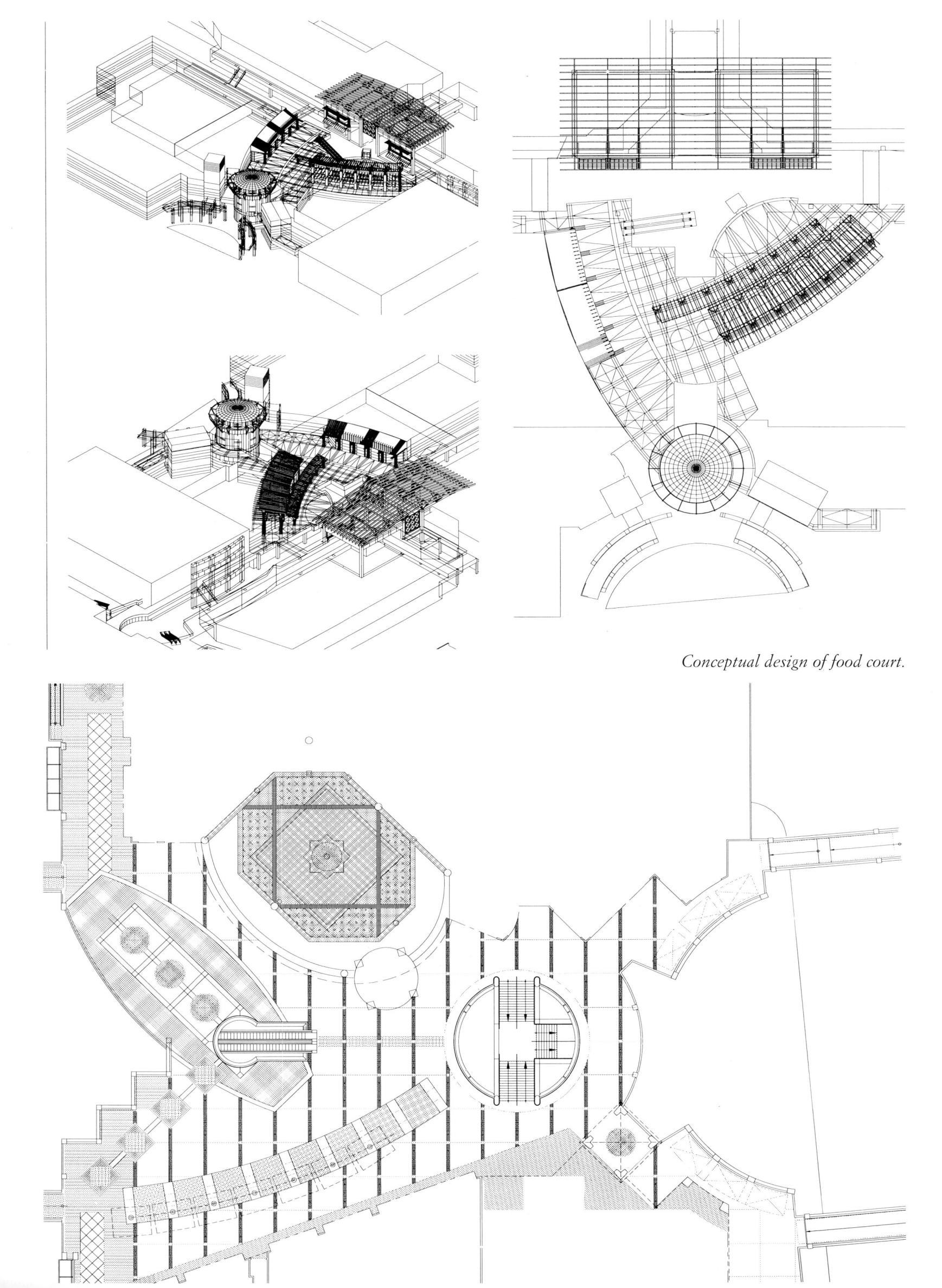

Conceptual design of food court.

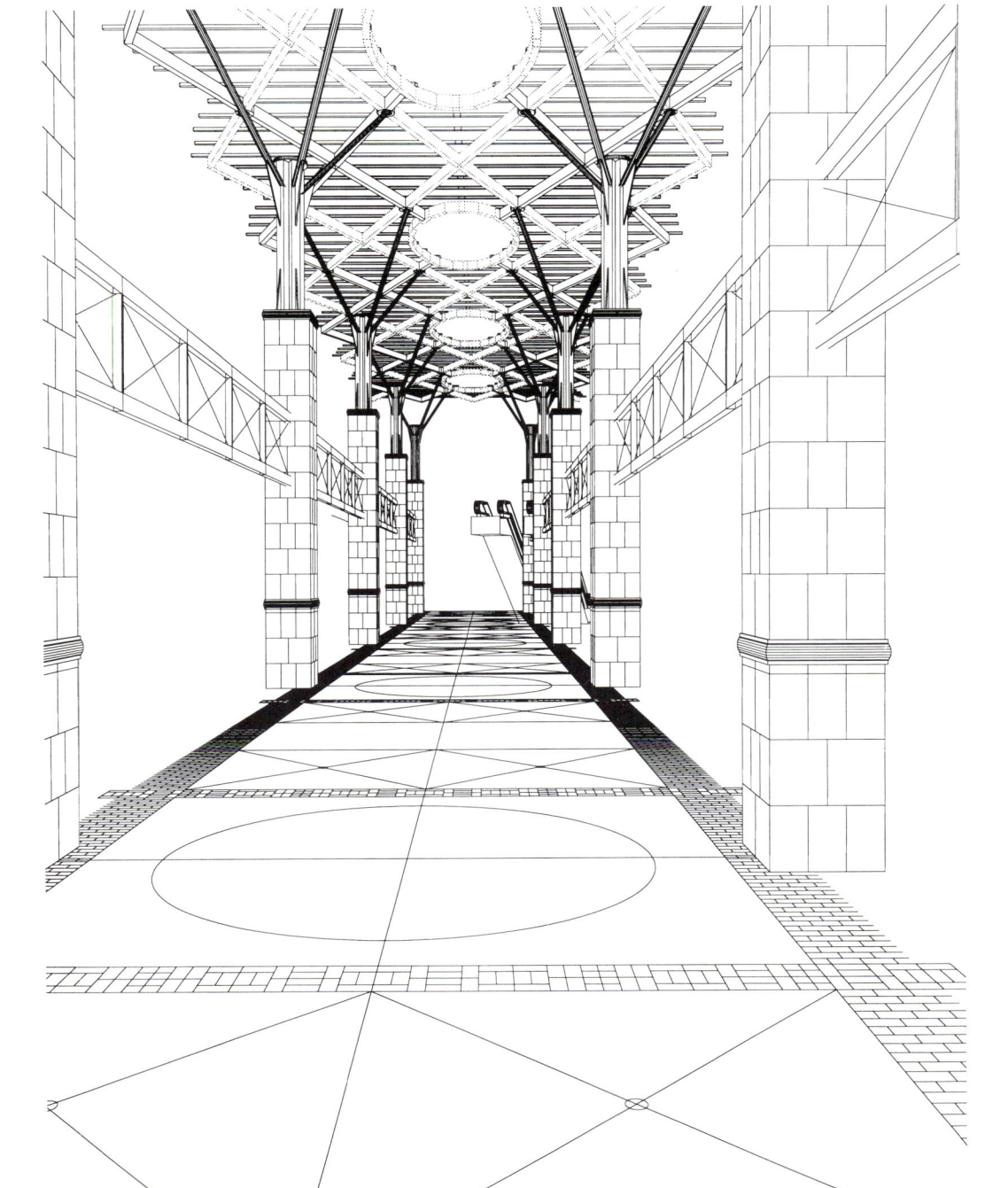

View of food court looking toward the portal structure.

Conceptual design of international court.

Views of portal structure.

Opposite page (counter clockwise from top), view looking west from portal structure; trellis canopy at walkway, and lantern column.

51

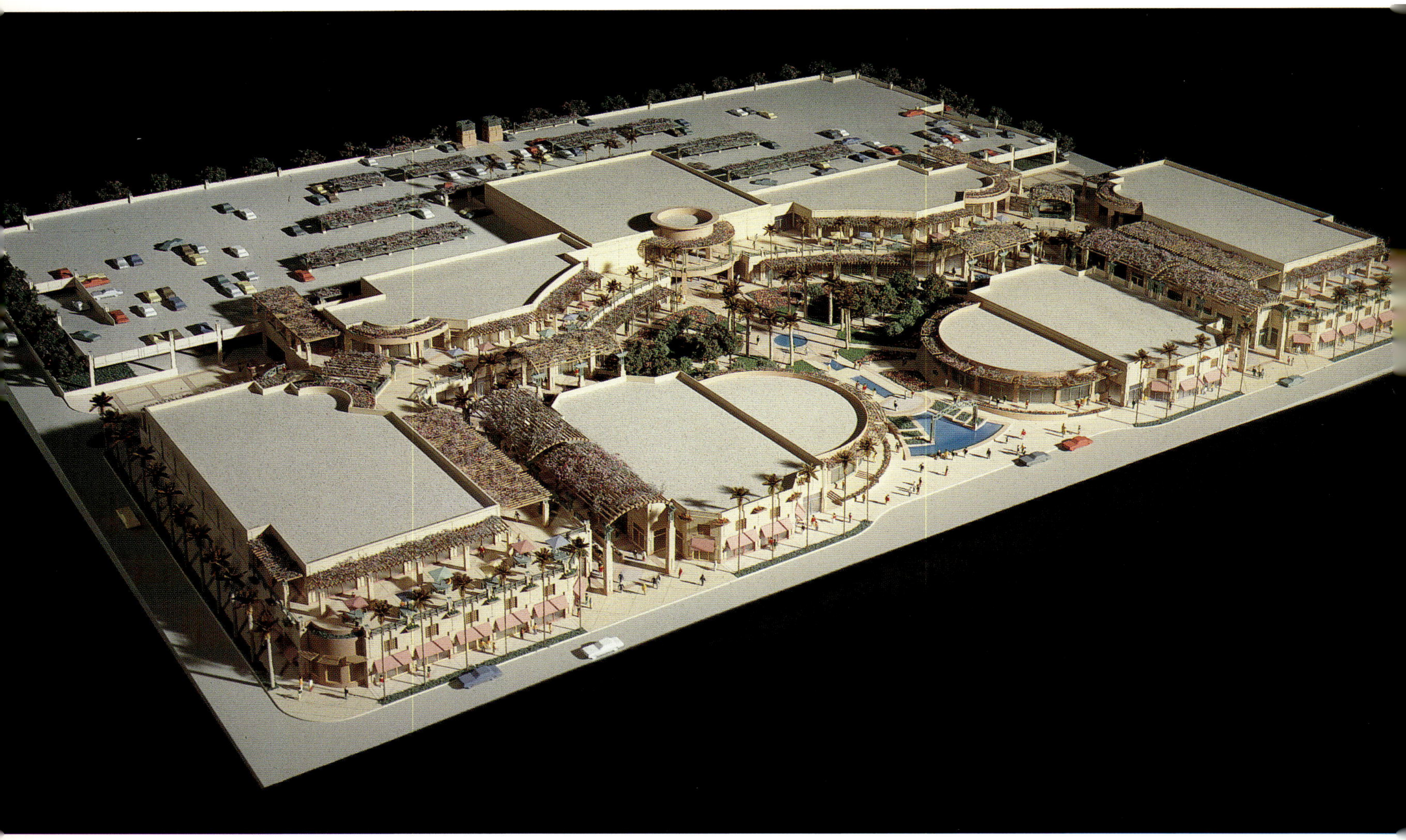

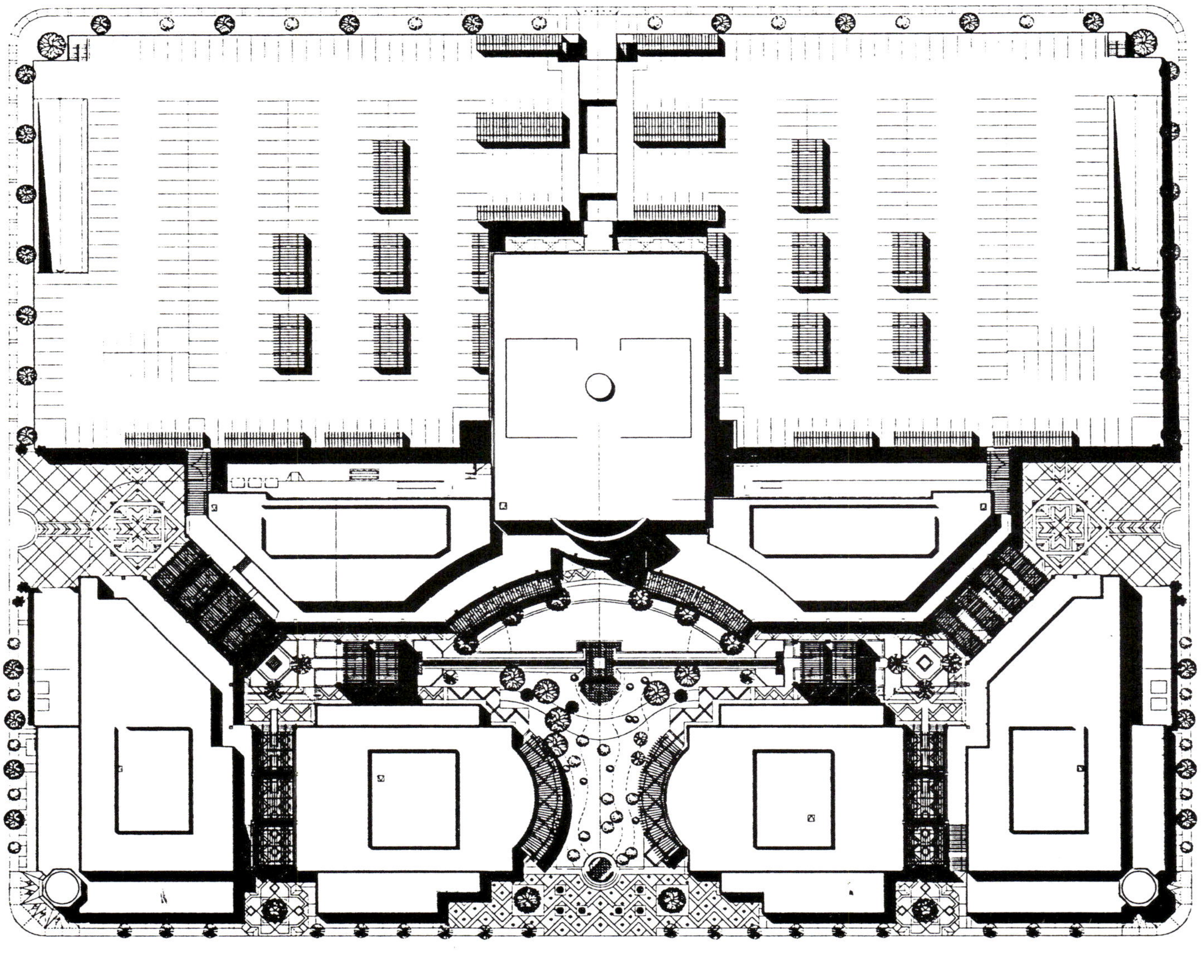

The Gardens on El Paseo

The Gardens on El Paseo, a modern, commercial complex with retail facilities and pedestrian amenities, is the new architectural landmark of Palm Desert's premier shopping district – a landscaped oasis in the arid climate. Located on the primary pedestrian street in Palm Desert, the project fills a gap in this one-mile stretch of commercial and retail properties. With the Gardens' design, Altoon + Porter Architects have created an anchor project that the street has been lacking, giving new allure to this prestigious address.

Conceived as an urban village, the facility reinforces the resort character of Palm Desert. The 207,000-square-foot, open-air complex consists of several two-level buildings including a 40,000-square-foot resort specialty store, 117,000 square feet of shops, and 50,000 square feet of upscale restaurants. The project contains a mix of uses that compliments the existing buildings in an architectural vocabulary appropriate to the surrounding environment.

The complex, a series of low-rise buildings placed along El Paseo, embraces the pedestrian activity along the commercial corridor. The main entrance is marked by a central sculpture that welcomes pedestrians into the complex. Several smaller entrances placed at intervals also draw pedestrians into the Gardens. The resort speciality store is located directly beyond the main entrance with additional upscale retail shops located on the ground levels of the surrounding buildings. An unobtrusive parking structure is placed at the far end of the site.

The two-level structures of the Gardens on El Paseo were designed as simple forms with refined detailing. Indigenous materials – plaster, stone, wood, and tile – add environmental context to the site. Rich earth colors evocative of sand, terra cotta, and sage coalesce to provide a contemporary setting distinguished by an understated elegance. These buildings are arranged in a classical composition that converges on a spacious and richly landscaped plaza, the site's spectacular centerpiece. Cafés, galleries, and outdoor restaurants are located on the second level of the buildings, allowing outdoor diners to survey the plaza activity from recessed terraces.

Against this architectural backdrop, a series of carefully arranged gardens, courts, and tranquil paseos with native flowering plants, palm trees, fountains, and lawns offer a unique shopping experience. Delicate trellis structures evocative of the sky interspersed with the more solid building forms anchored in the earth create a dialogue that gives a quiet sense of formal order to this engaging pedestrian environment.

Altoon + Porter stressed continuity with the surrounding neighborhood in its design of the Gardens on El Paseo. By incorporating local, recognizable materials and creating a complex to match the elegance of an already established shopping tract, the firm added a new source of pride and an elevated stature to the community.

Aerial overview, and below, building detail.

View along main thoroughfare, and below, the central axis.

56

Bighorn Institute

As in many of Altoon + Porter's earlier projects, the driving force behind the Bighorn Institute's design was to create a place suited to the local population. What made this project unusual, was that a big part of the population would not be human but animal – the bighorn sheep.

Long endangered, the bighorn sheep have a mortality rate as high as 97 percent. The Bighorn Institute in Palm Desert, the only organization in the United States licensed to care for the sheep, is dedicated to the conservation of the animals and the creation of public awareness about the steady decline of the sheep population.

Altoon + Porter was commissioned by the Bighorn Institute to help carry out its mission through the design of a multi-use compound. To be built in three phases, the program for the institute included a dedicated animal hospital and study laboratory for the pathology of the disease, a residential facility for the scientists who are on site 24-hours a day, and a museum designed to educate the public regarding the animals' plight.

While the project type was new for Altoon + Porter, the project approach was proven. In keeping with the firm's commitment to context-linked solutions, the architects' search for an appropriate metaphor led to the traditional desert shelter – the caravanserai.

Historically, the caravanserai was a walled compound that provided shelter for travelers crossing the desert. It was a secure place for replenishing supplies, repairing the body, and soothing the soul. Like the caravanserai, the Bighorn Institute was to be a sanctuary where the endangered sheep could find protection and care.

Such duality of purpose – that of animal care and public outreach – required a facility that was flexible. Not only did it have to be designed to provide for the sheep, but it had to create a sense of private living space for the scientists. Visually and functionally, the Bighorn Institute had to be distinctive enough to invite and keep public interest. It needed to be an icon for the cause.

Selected for its isolation, the institute's desert location is, by its nature, a fragile environment. Both animal and human inhabitants, depend on a delicate balance of factors that enable them to survive. But the construction of the Bighorn Institute would, to a certain extent, threaten the natural environment. Knowing this, Altoon + Porter used the design to mitigate the potential damage in several ways. First, the educational component of the Bighorn Institute, the museum, serves as both a gateway and a barrier. Dedicated to increasing awareness, the museum is deliberately sited to give full protection to all the living creatures on the preserve. Second, the use of materials reflects the desert's forms and colors, allowing the structures to blend into the natural domain. The massing of the building is layered against itself in the same way that the mountains appear to be layered against themselves. As the first component of the institute to be built, the residence borrows the vocabulary of the native adobe – exceptionally thick walls, high ceilings, and ample lighting from the clerestories – that neutralizes the high temperatures of the arid desert.

Located at the end of a quarter arch on the northern side of the compound, the residential area includes 4,100 square feet of living area and parking. The building itself centers around a boardroom designed for group functions and discussions. Surrounding the common area are the sleeping quarters. Although the sheep receive constant attention from the on-site scientists, the humans involved in this community needed a place of their own for respite and privacy.

But the purpose of the compound as a whole still focuses on the animals. Today, the boardroom doubles as an operating room for the sheep until the institute is completed. And until the hospital and museum become realities, the residential area will continue taking on many ad hoc uses.

Exterior view and trellis detail.

Site plan and, below, residence floor plan.

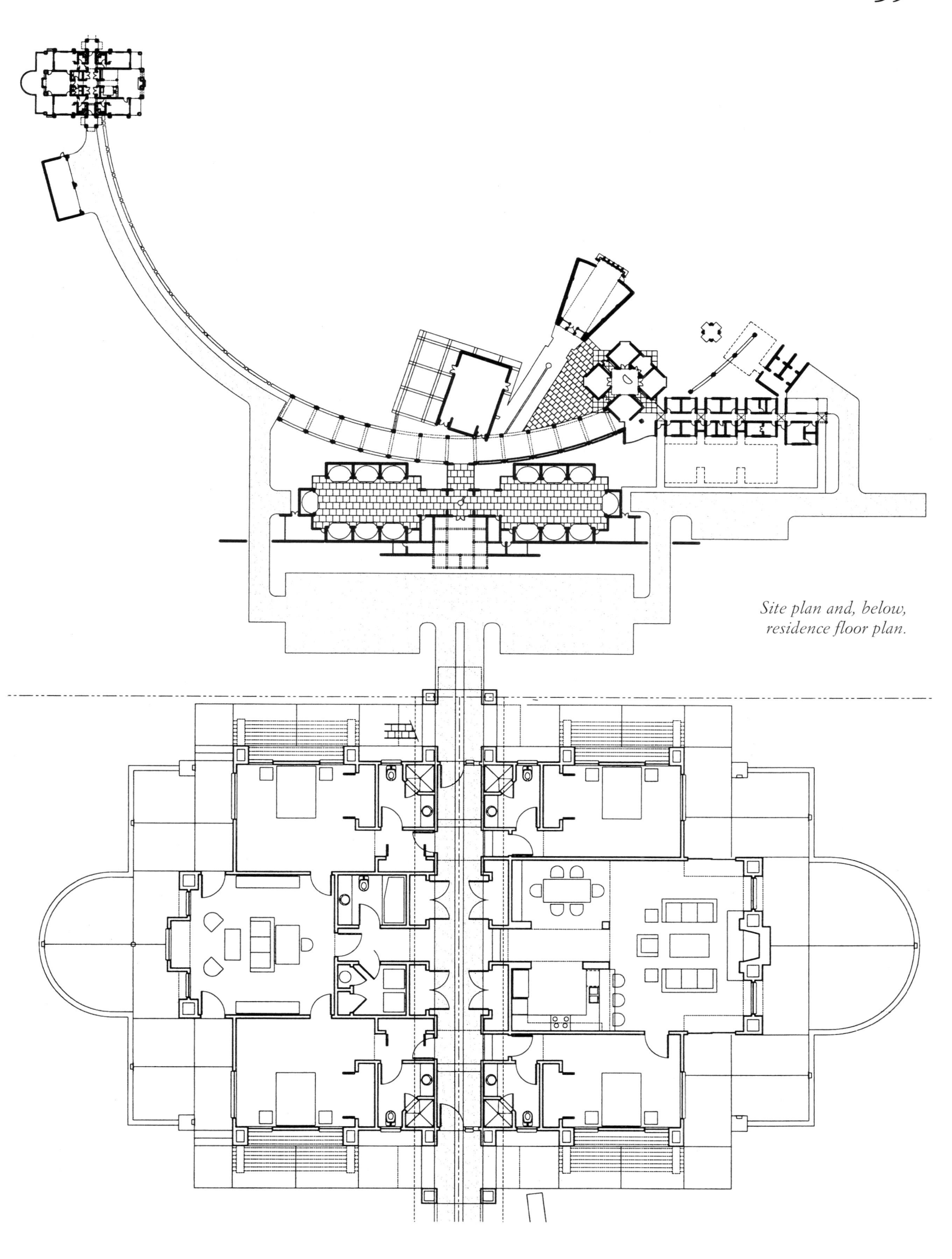

View of the institute in its context.

Twilight view.

62

Siqueiros Mural Shade Structure

When the Getty Conservation Institute sought to save a historic outdoor mural in downtown Los Angeles, Altoon + Porter Architects was commissioned to design a structure that would protect the work from future environmental damage. The mural, "America Tropical," was completed by David Alfaro Siqueiros in 1932 on the site of the city's original Latino settlement. A controversial project from its inception, the mural has remained a sacred icon for the city's Latino community. Altoon + Porter designed a protective, unimposing shelter that would give the mural a dignified place of honor within its historic setting.

The shade structure is an innovative design that combines the latest technology with an intense respect for a significant work of art. Painted on a second-story wall adjacent to a former rooftop beer garden, Siqueiros's mural depicts the suffering of natives at the hands of newly-arrived missionaries. At the time, the artist's virtuoso treatment of sensitive social issues was considered volatile and the mural was whitewashed the day it was unveiled. But its message resonated with the native Hispanics who saw the truth of their personal experience reflected in Siqueiros's artwork.

Following 62 years of neglect, seismic damage, and exposure to ultraviolet rays, the mural had fallen into a critical state of disrepair. As part of the restoration project, the Getty Conservation Institute wanted to create a setting for education and public events while preserving the work for many years to come. To serve the larger educational purposes of the project, the structure was designed to contain seating and audio visual equipment, including a projection screen. Perimeter ramps would allow wheelchair access within 10 feet of the mural. The most important requirement was that the mural remain accessible to the public at all times and be completely visible up close and from a distance.

The concept was to craft a structure that employs diffused light to enhance the original intent of the work while mitigating environmental effects. To meet these goals, the initial design process included careful studies of weather and sun exposure. Both the Getty Conservation Institute and Altoon + Porter carried out extensive research on the potential climatic effects. A monitoring station installed next to the mural measured wind speed and direction, rainfall, temperature, humidity, and the sun's movement.

In essence, the design solution is a high-tech shrine that re-integrates the mural with its context. Access to the artwork would be facilitated by a stairway and elevator from the commercially active Olvera Street, and by a bridge offering an uninterrupted view of the entire mural. As a self-ventilating, fabric canopy, the shade structure would rise above the mural and cover the rooftop area. Rotating vertical scrims on a steel supporting system were designed to bow down gently to shield the mural from all ultraviolet rays, almost all heat, and even the low winter sun. The mural would be illuminated by diffused, filtered light to enhance its visibility. During the day, Teflon-coated fiberglass has a shimmering, translucent quality. At night, it glows under soft artificial light which would allow nighttime viewing.

The new context was designed to create an outdoor museum that connects visitors with Siqueiros's vision, the heritage of the Americas, and the city's origins, making the structure a respectful addition to the festive spirit and historic background of Olvera Street. With its new setting, "America Tropical" would regain its status as a important cultural artifact.

Altoon + Porter's shade structure was conceived to not only protect a deteriorating masterpiece from the harsh exterior environment, but also to enable the mural to be enjoyed by present and future visitors. Its unusual and innovative design pays homage to the spirit and intent of the artist, his art, and the vibrant community of Los Angeles.

Section, elevation and perspective views.

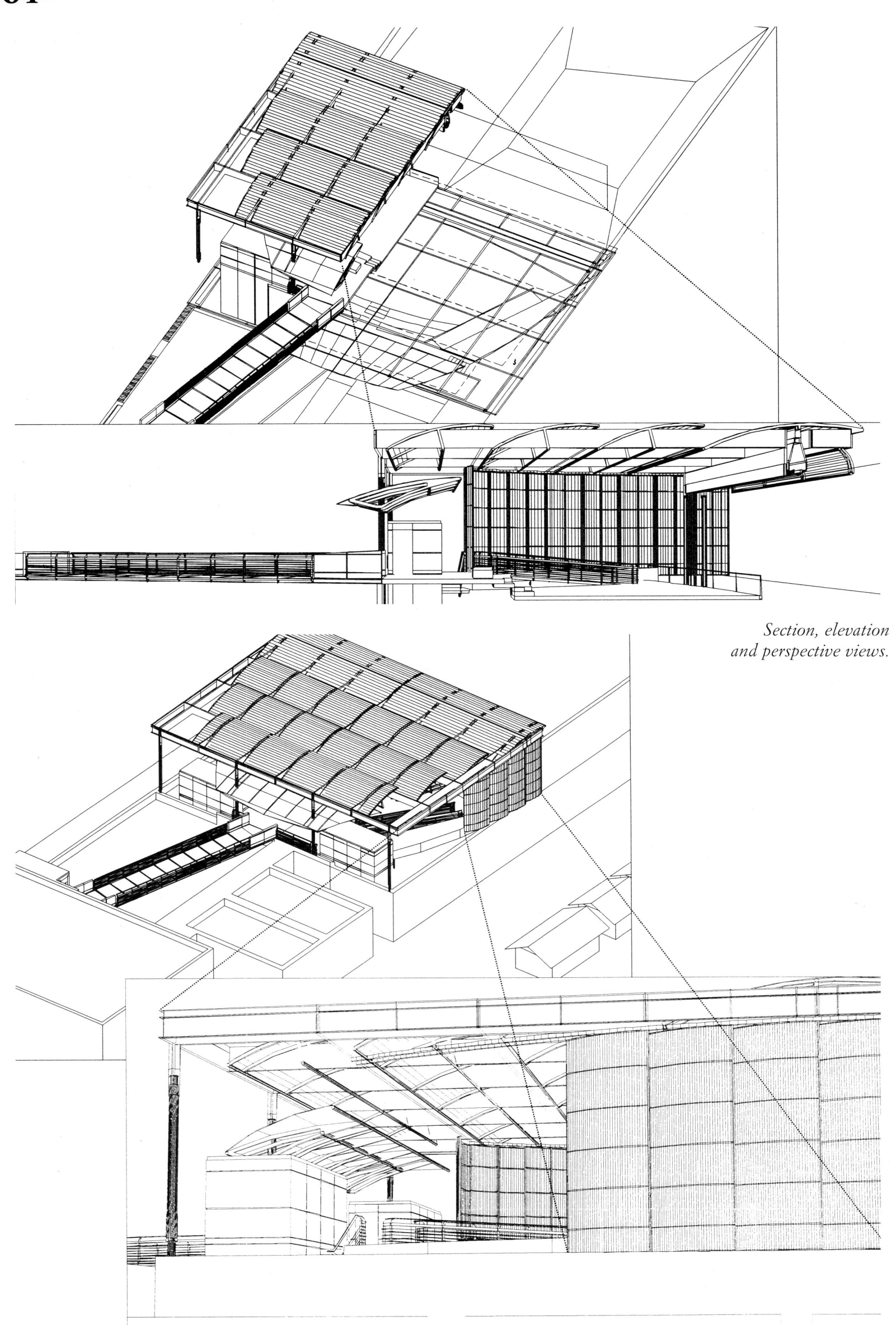

View from the bridge.

View of the mural from the viewing platform.

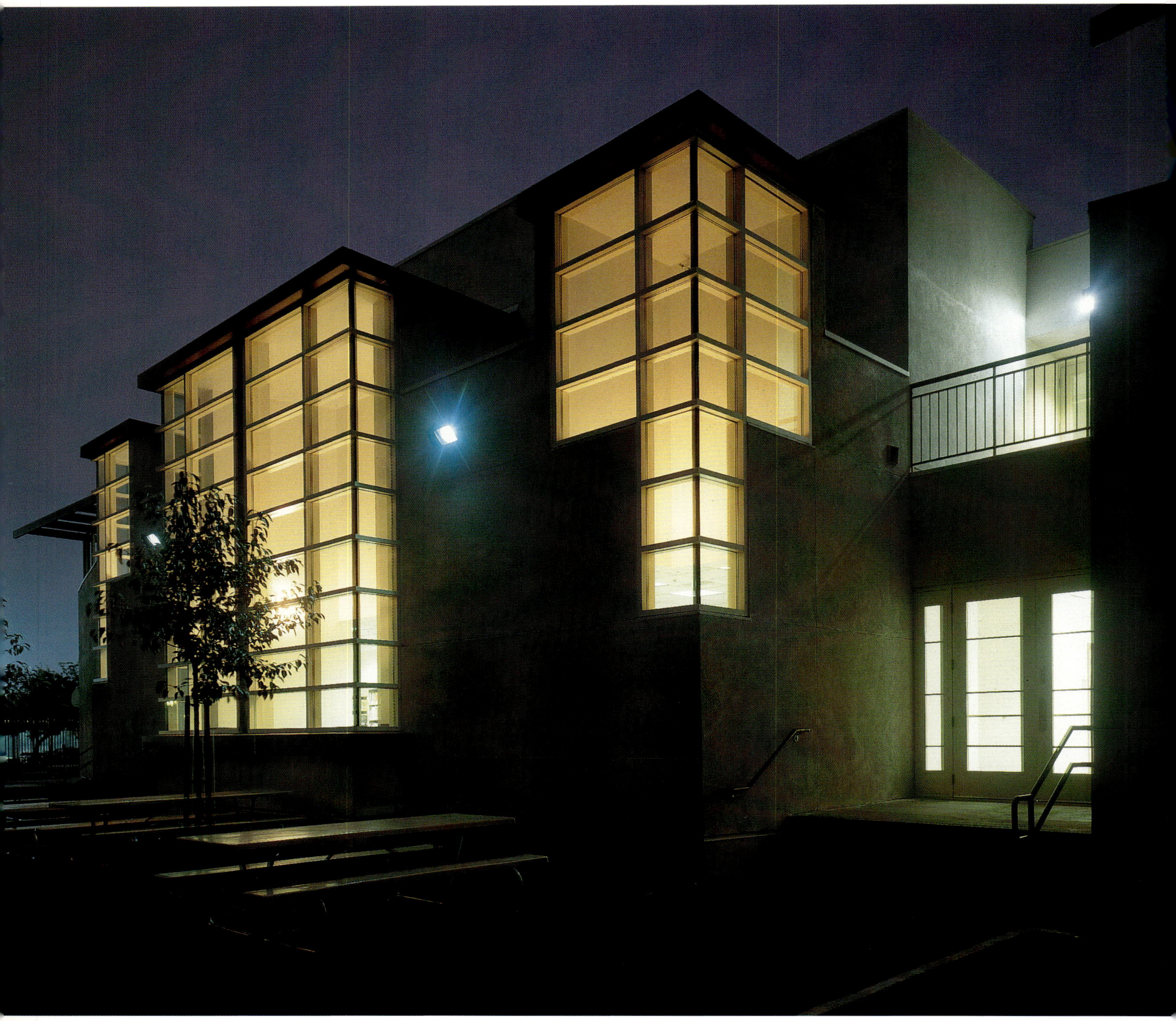

Echo/Horizon School

For almost 30 years, the mission of the Echo/Horizon School, a private K-6 school in Culver City, California, has been to educate hearing impaired children in an environment that does not isolate them from hearing students. When the school outgrew the confines of its space, the administration commissioned Altoon + Porter Architects to renovate and expand the facility.

Built in 1926, the existing buildings were architecturally undistinguished, "formula" buildings, but the old school held sentimental attachments for the community. In fact, the city designated the original school as a "significant" local structure. Despite its nostalgic value to the city, the building's immediate neighbors had long complained about the school's auditorium, whose posterior fronted the residential area. The creation of a positive new face to compliment the residential neighborhood was one of the primary challenges for the architectural team.

Like many Los Angeles area buildings, the school was rebuilt after being severely damaged by the Long Beach Earthquake of 1933 and suffered structural damage again in the 1987 Whittier Earthquake. Therefore, seismic upgrading was part of the program.

The school required expansion space for eight new classrooms – including an art and music room and a computer lab – as well as a library and outdoor play yards, all on a very tight site. The design solution recalls the mission of the school itself: avoid separation, integrate. Thus, the approach for Echo/Horizon treated the additions as attachments to the original building.

Acting as a "cloak" that envelopes the north, east, and south sides of the building, the new, wraparound wing is formal in composition, strengthening the school's sense of institution. The use of stucco, metal, and glass – materials of the original structure – creates continuity between the old building and the new. While the materials were compatible with the existing palette, they were distinctive enough to establish a new identity and improve the image of the school.

For the hearing impaired, the visual environment takes on increased importance. The design offsets the emphasis on hearing and concentrates on visual appeal and the use of light. The new library was designed with a large bay window with stepped-up seating so children can sit in the light and enjoy being read to by their teacher.

Making a place for new tools was equally important. New lighting and computer network capabilities were installed. The computer lab was located in one of the classrooms adjacent to the library, allowing an ability to share Internet resources between lab and library.

Working within a limited budget, the architects effectively minimized the costs of maintaining four separate buildings by centralizing all of the various functions. And, as importantly, the school sent out a positive community image by providing a friendly façade. With a new face and a new message, Echo/Horizon School makes a powerful statement without a need for words.

View of commons area.

View of stair corner.

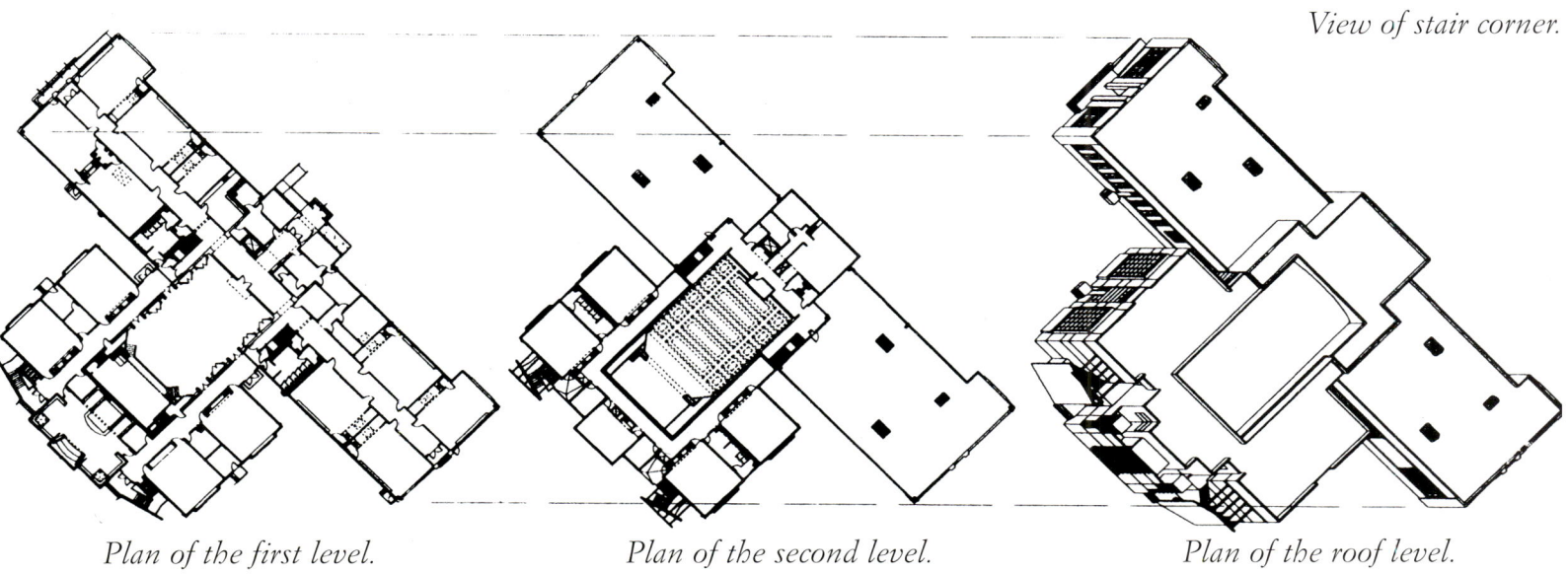

Plan of the first level. *Plan of the second level.* *Plan of the roof level.*

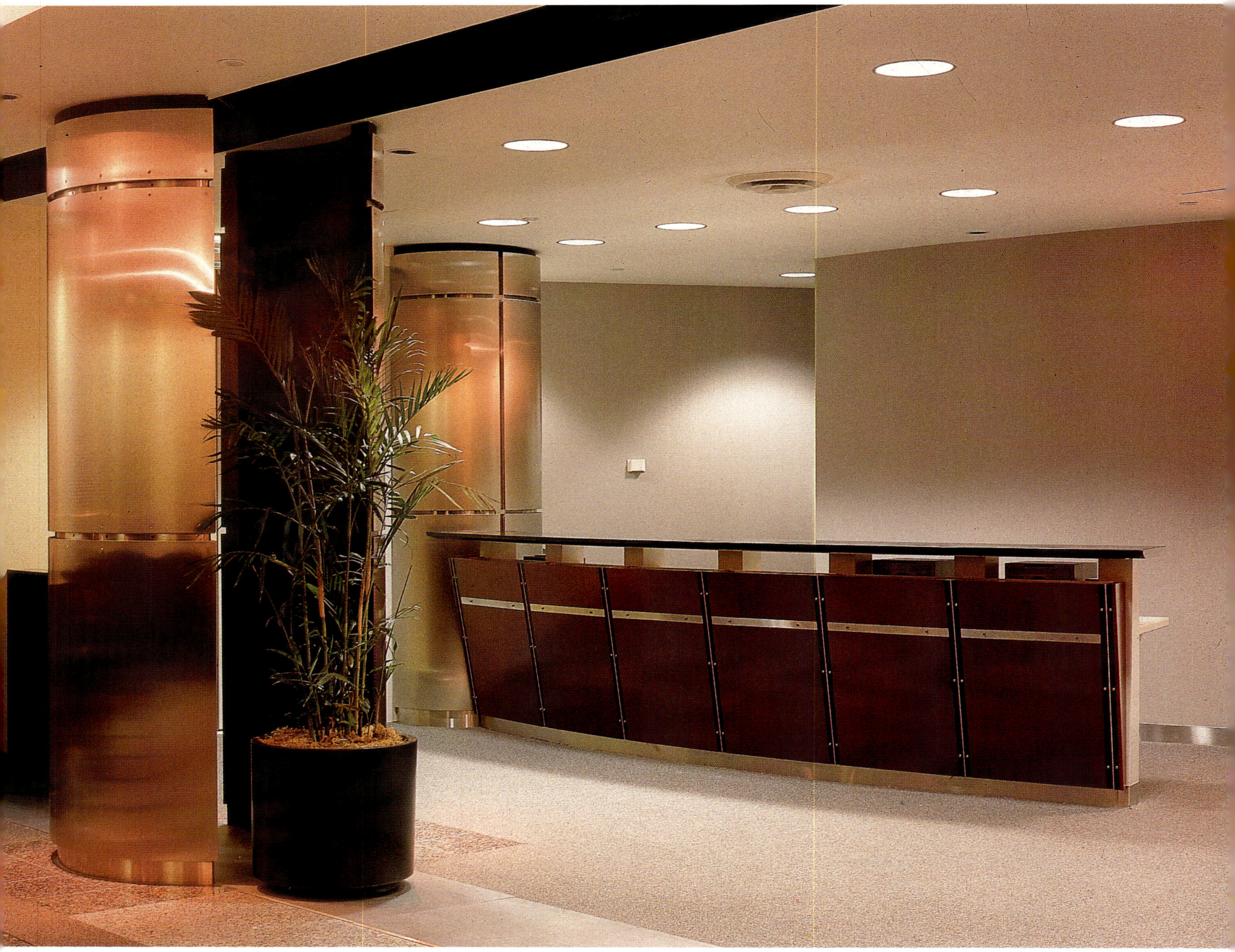

MCA Employee Services

The success of MCA Universal Studios' CityWalk entertainment complex created a need for a new home for the creative staff. However, it was hard to imagine leaving the campus where each building and each group had its own distinctive identity in its own building (including some in trailers on the old movie lot). MCA decided to consolidate its headquarters into one building where executives, accounting, training, uniforms claims, ride operations, merchandising, food services, television development, corporate sponsorship, and planning and development (recreational services) would all live together like a family.

Moving these highly creative individuals (and some of their familiar, old props including the hand from King Kong and a Fred Flintstone statue from the Flintstones movie) to a conventional office environment required an unconventional design approach. Enter Altoon + Porter Architects. Charged with creating an environment that would give order to the newly consolidated organization and leave room for individual identities, the architects gave each floor a very different character, but used shared elements to unify the whole. In order to create points of difference, the elements of the interior architecture were abstracted. Individual architectural components – columns, ceilings, walls – are featured to surprise workers and visitors alike, belying the conventional nature of the office space.

Each of the six office lobbies is characterized by an orientation space with its own reception desk leading to a secondary space accessed by a racetrack that loops around the central common area. This racetrack circulation system allows entrances for the various departments to take on their own identity – to metaphorically hang their "shingle" outside of their place of business. In addition, each floor has its own conference room, restrooms, and kitchen facilities.

Space, as it is experienced in the MCA headquarters, is a study in difference. Angular, circular, oblong, and irregular spaces with their pronounced details speak to the occupants of this big, "fun" house. For Altoon + Porter, the project proved that their aesthetic play with elements and details worked as well in the narrow confines of the speculative office environment as in their larger, commercial complexes.

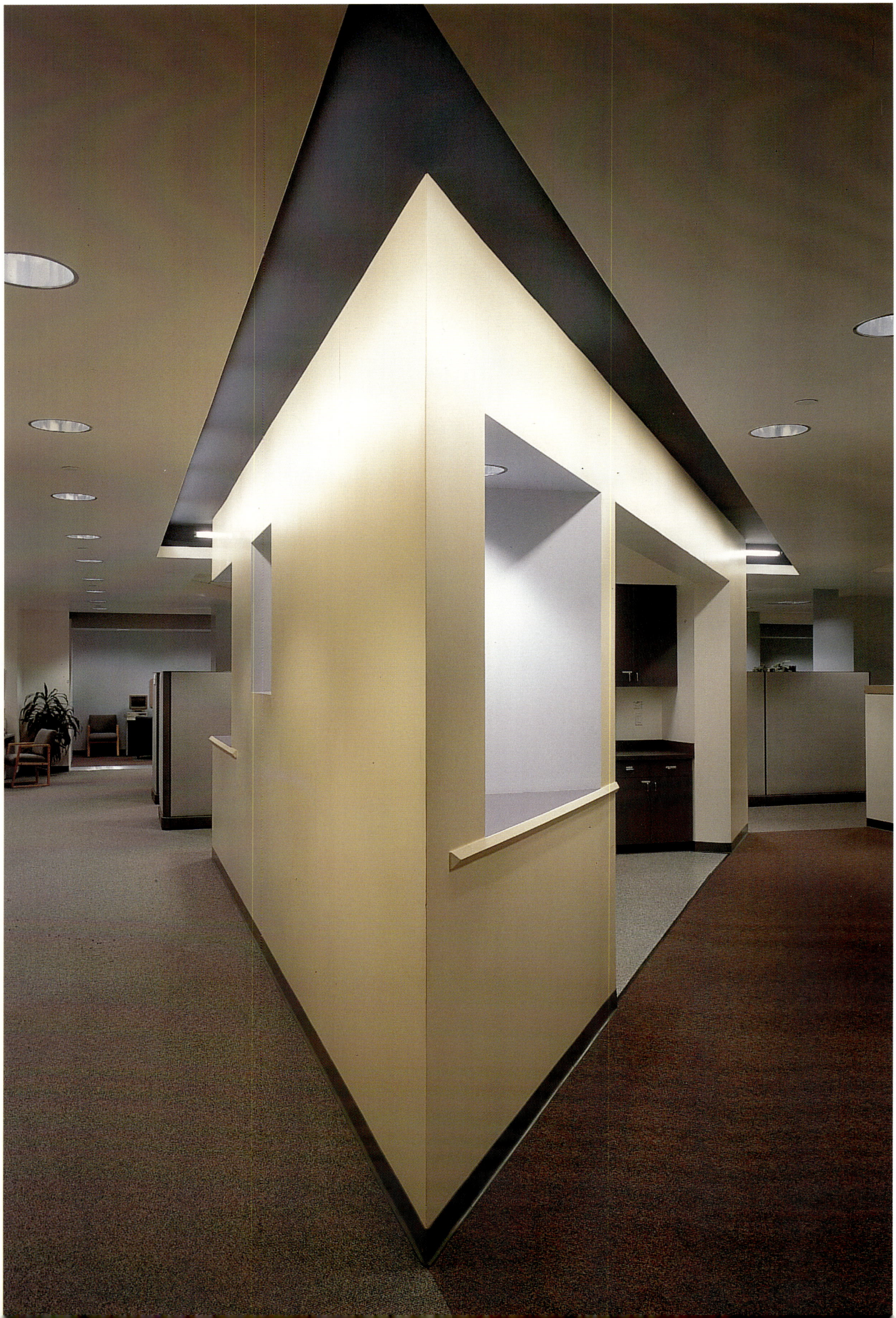

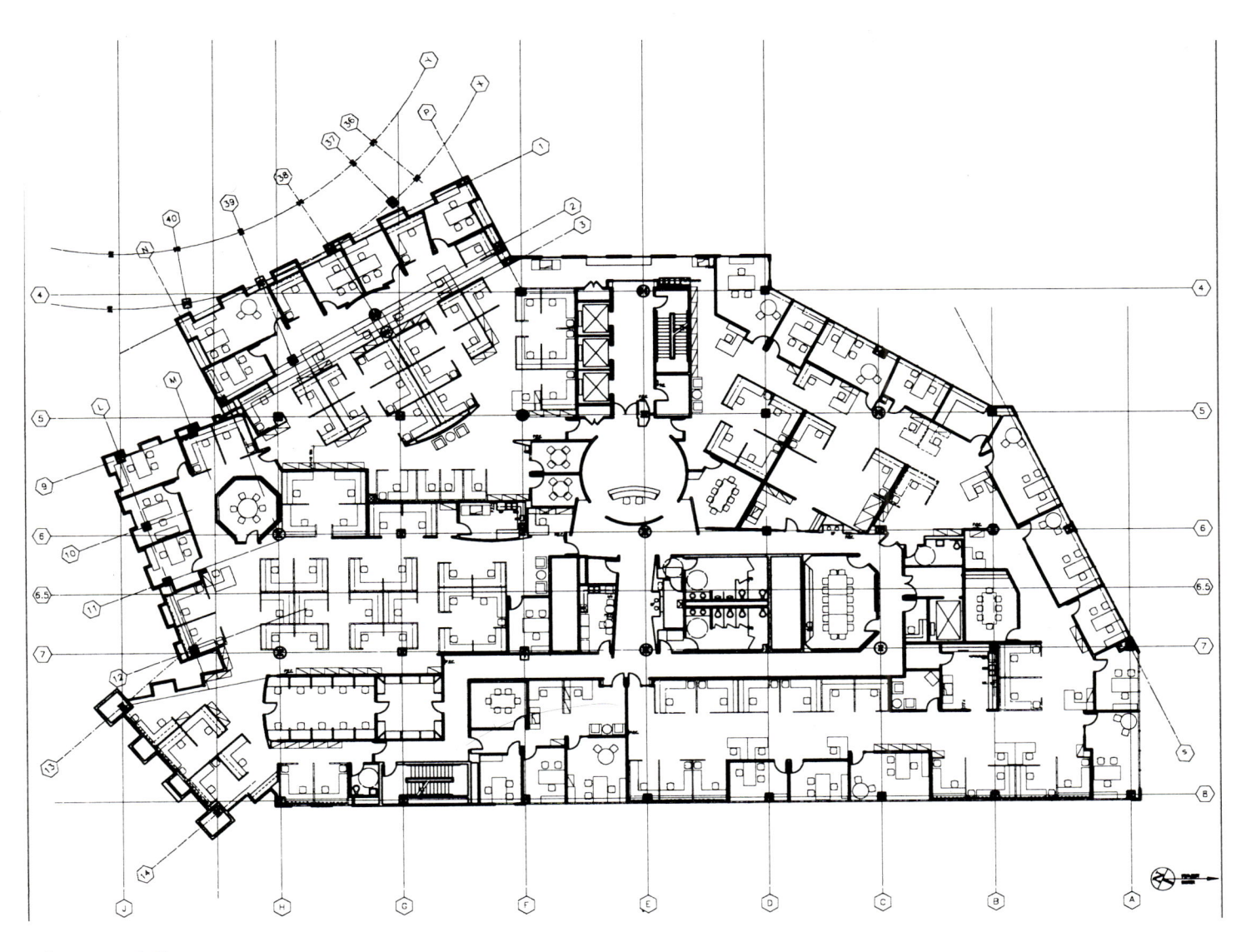

Plan of a typical floor.
Right, the reception at fifth level.
Opposite page, interior building detail.

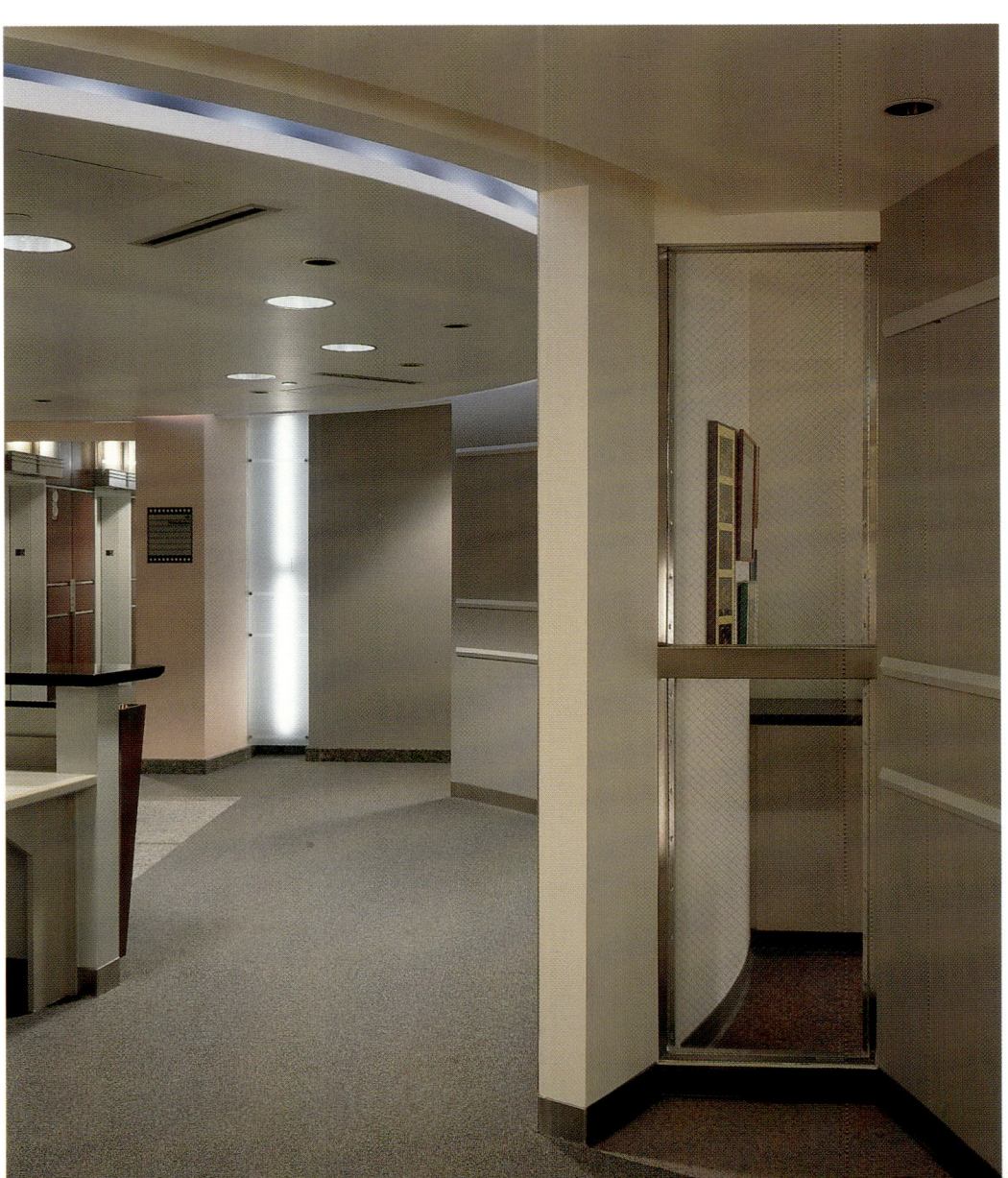

Below, view from the elevator hall toward reception area. Opposite page, clockwise from top left, detail of the call lantern, detail of the corridor, and typical display panels.

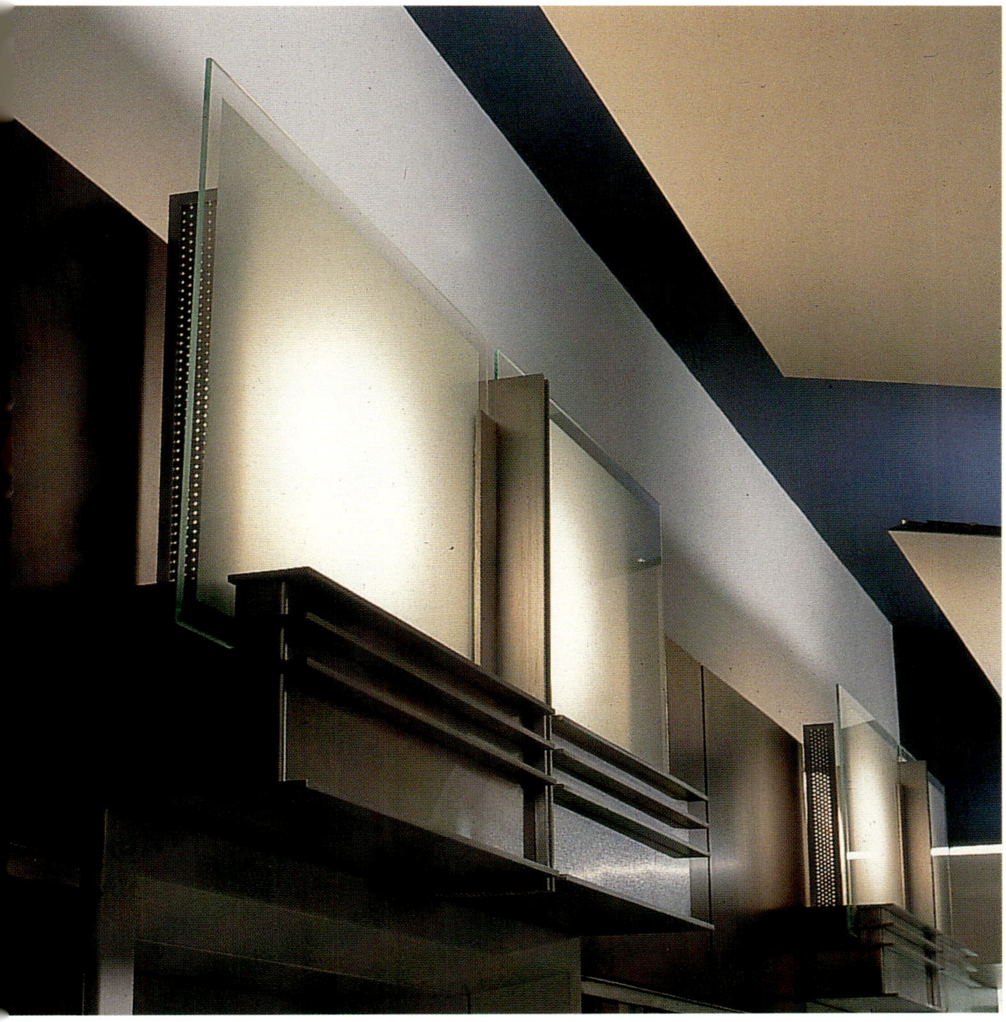

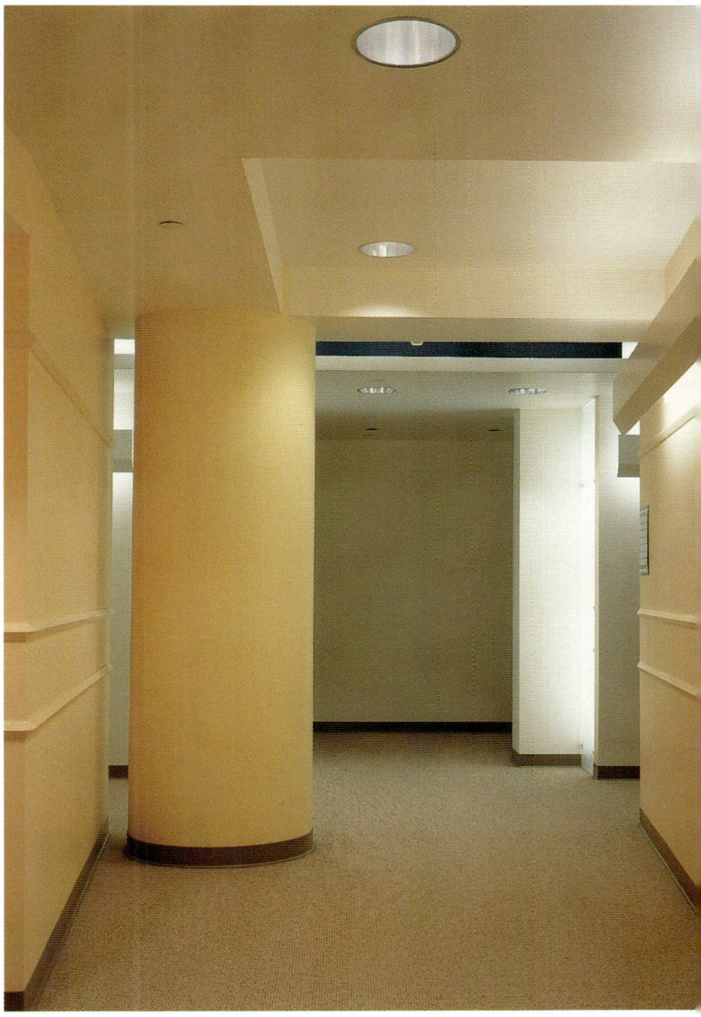

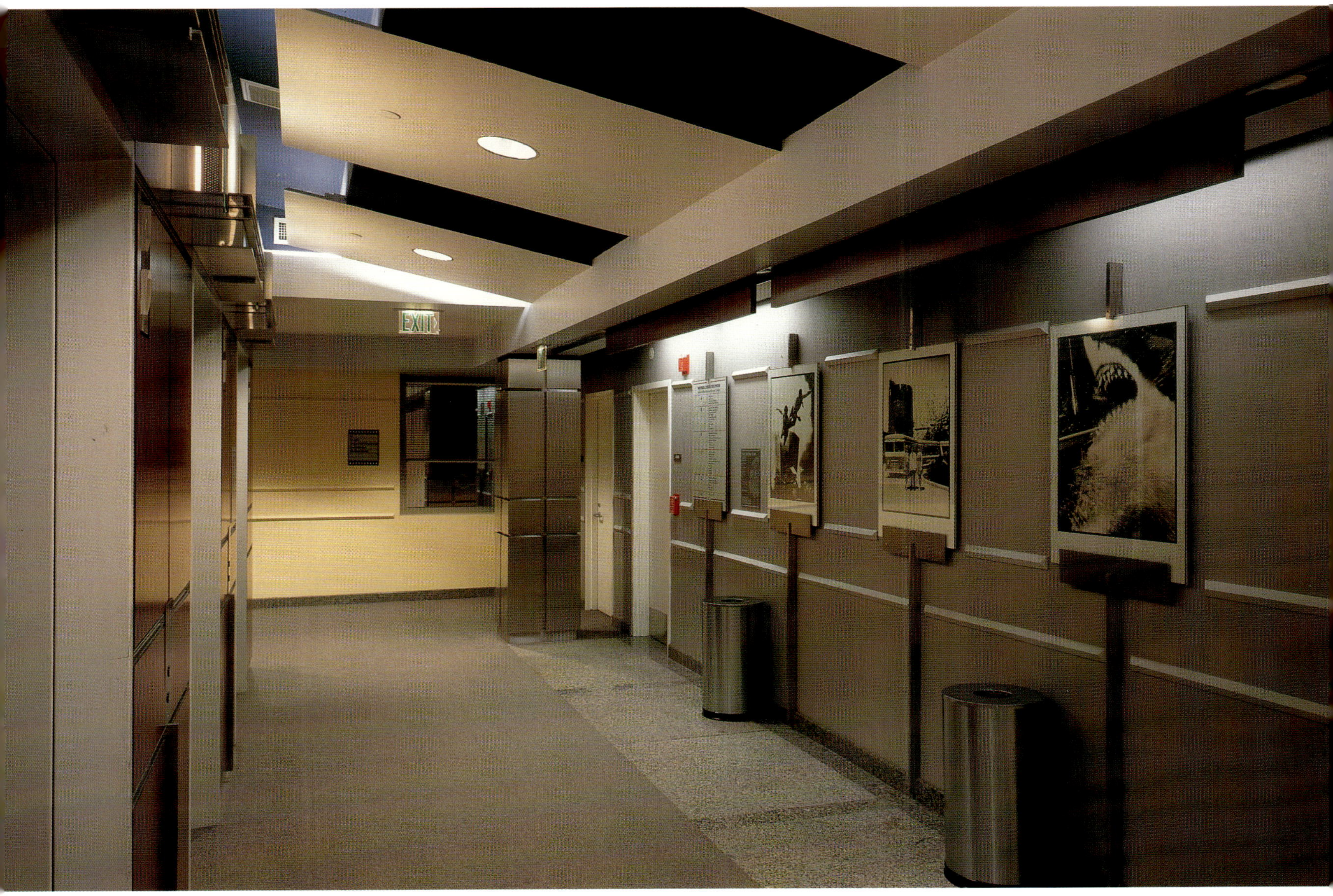
EXIT

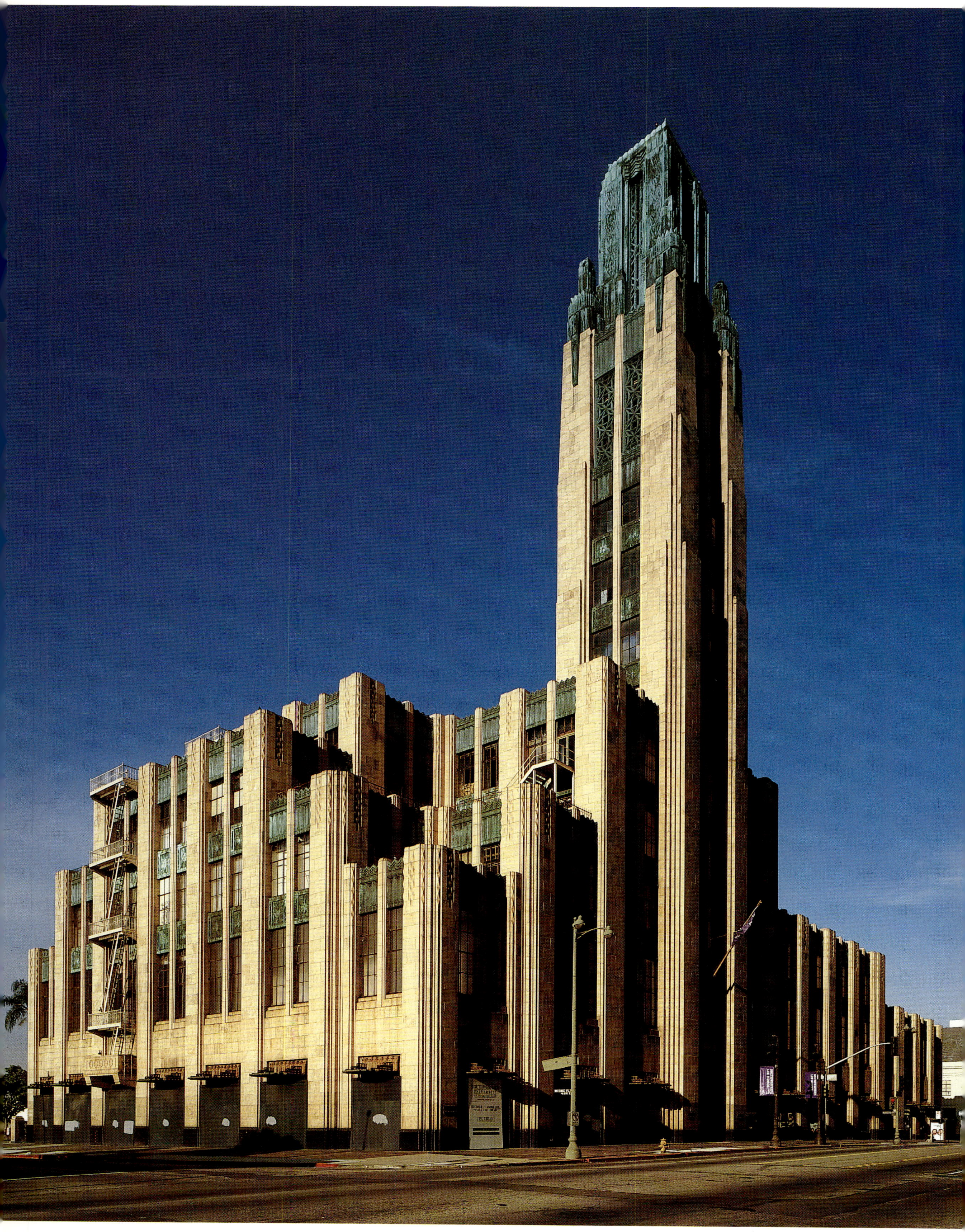

Southwestern University School of Law

When the 1929 Bullock's Wilshire building, a Los Angeles landmark that had come to symbolize the optimism and glamour of old Hollywood, became available, Altoon + Porter Architects were at work on a new law library for Southwestern University Law School. The firm had already prepared plans for expansion to a neighboring block, but Altoon + Porter was convinced that Bullock's Wilshire would serve the school well, both as a recognizable icon, and as an accommodating space for the library's needs. The firm boldly changed plans and began carefully refitting the old building to meet a modern agenda.

Historic properties always present a dual challenge. With the Bullock's Wilshire building, the challenge was to create an ideal place for study and research for Southwestern students and, at the same time, restore the most significant of the famed interiors to their original condition. The architects believed that the fabled murals and original woodwork should continue to grace the facility, while modern necessities should be added to ensure that Southwestern could continue to provide a quality legal education. Cutting-edge technology, computer labs, study rooms, networked seating, and open book stacks had to be incorporated into the existing facility.

To maintain the balance of interests, Altoon + Porter assigned two project architects – one to handle historic preservation, and one to provide for the client's updated needs. The first concern, the restoration process, was mostly archaeological. With over 65 years of continual use, substantial deviations from the initial design had occurred. Meanwhile the historic component of the approval process mandated that the building be brought back to the most "original" state possible. Altoon + Porter consulted with local preservationists and the city's Cultural Heritage Commission, and also researched collections of historic and photographic data to reveal hidden, early design elements. The results were recorded on different CAD layers, ranging from the first architect's 1928 shell and core to the conditions found in 1995. The architects restored the original features of the building as they upgraded the mechanical systems including fire alarms, plumbing, and heating and cooling. They also made the facility completely handicapped accessible.

The second concern was to adapt a complex and comprehensive library program in a manner that respected the store's original layout. Altoon + Porter's design capitalized on the compartmental format, where specialty boutiques linked rooms of distinct character, color, and materials. The new plan provided for the stacking of 365,000 volumes, while the functional organization honored the integrity of the individual departments of the former store. Furthermore, the plan created adequate seating and study carrels and a computer network that allows students to plug in a laptop computer and access the library's resources from any room.

Patrons access the library from a gracious foyer leading to the Perfume Hall to find an exquisite Art Deco hall veneered in rose and marble, and ceiling frescos by Herman Sachs. Serving as the central axis of the building, this area is reserved for reception and orientation. Altoon + Porter added new circulation elements as well.

Design cues were taken from the furniture and functional uses of the existing rooms. Custom wood bookcases, with warm tones and patterns reminiscent of the block houses of Frank Lloyd Wright, recall the original character of the clothing display racks in the former menswear department. The balcony at the mezzanine level was opened up to recreate the modernist play of space and form, and previously hidden elements, such as the original brick flooring of the former Riding Shop, were recovered.

The new library successfully blends the past with the present. The historic nature of the building was preserved and enhanced with state-of-the-art technology and functional, exciting design to create a dynamic learning and research facility befitting Southwestern University. And Los Angeles' beloved "Cathedral Of Commerce" is back in business, building a new legacy with students instead of starlets.

View toward the library.

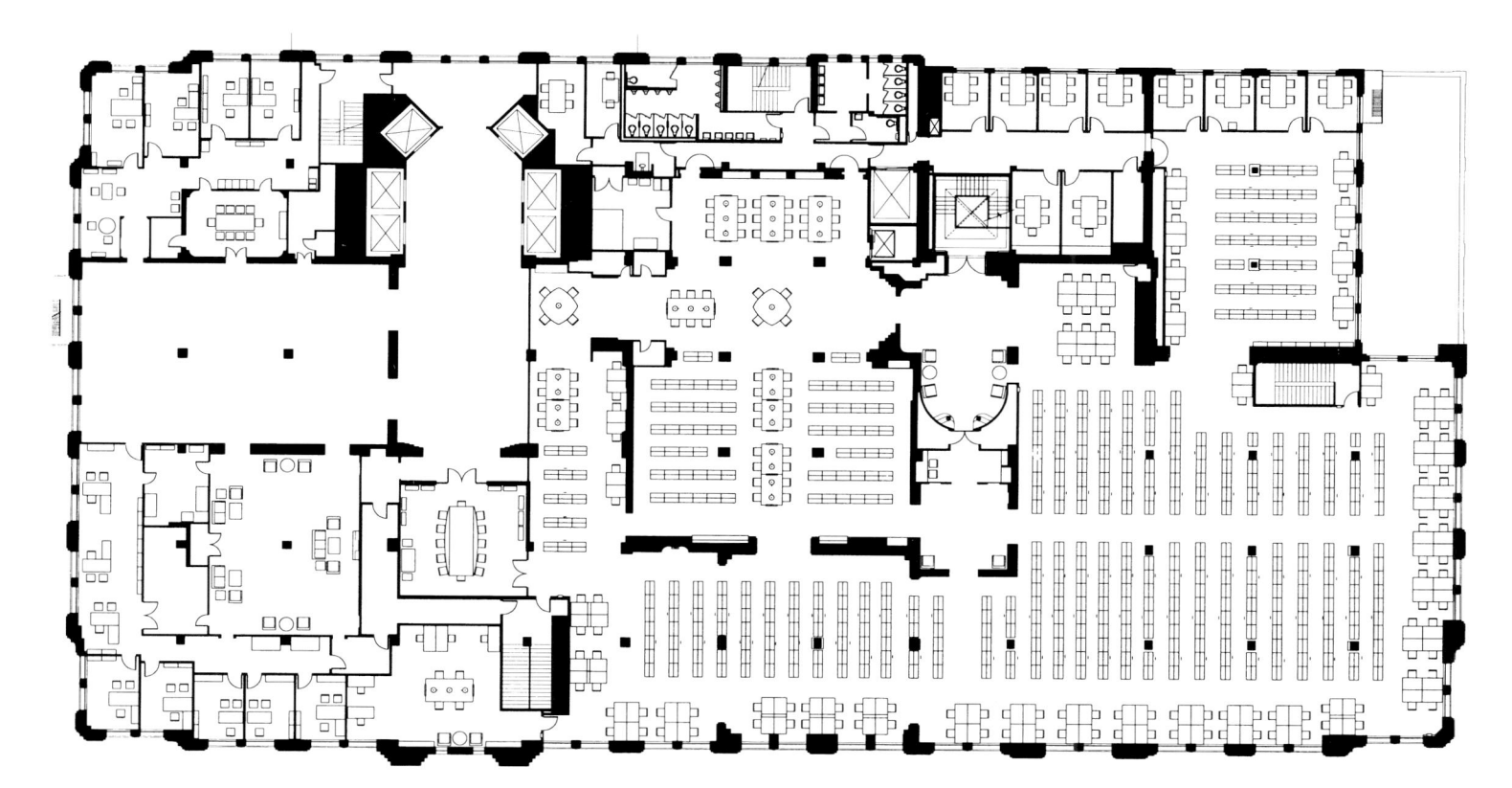

Plan of the second floor.

Plan of the ground floor.

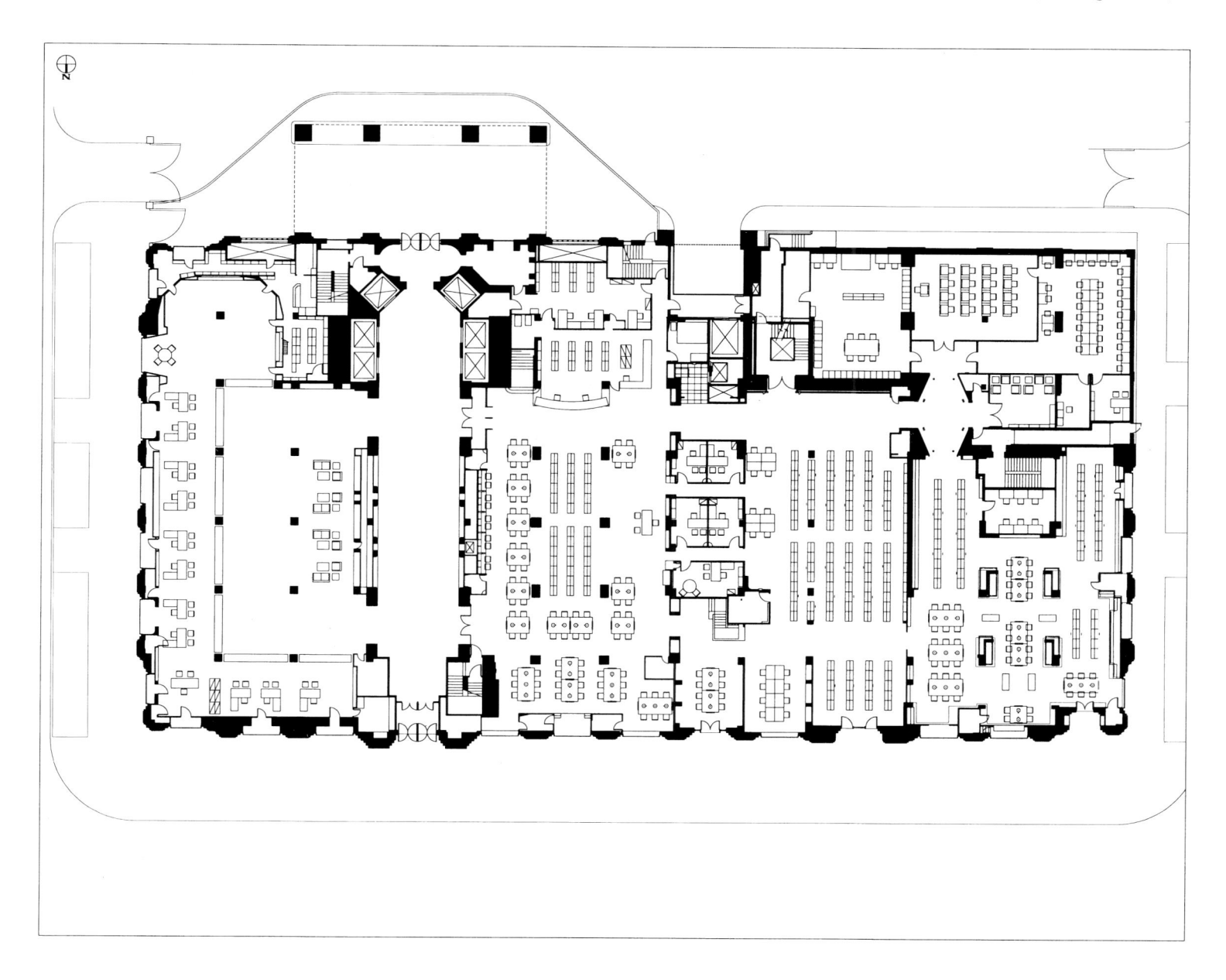

New circulating stair.

Elevator hall and library entrance.

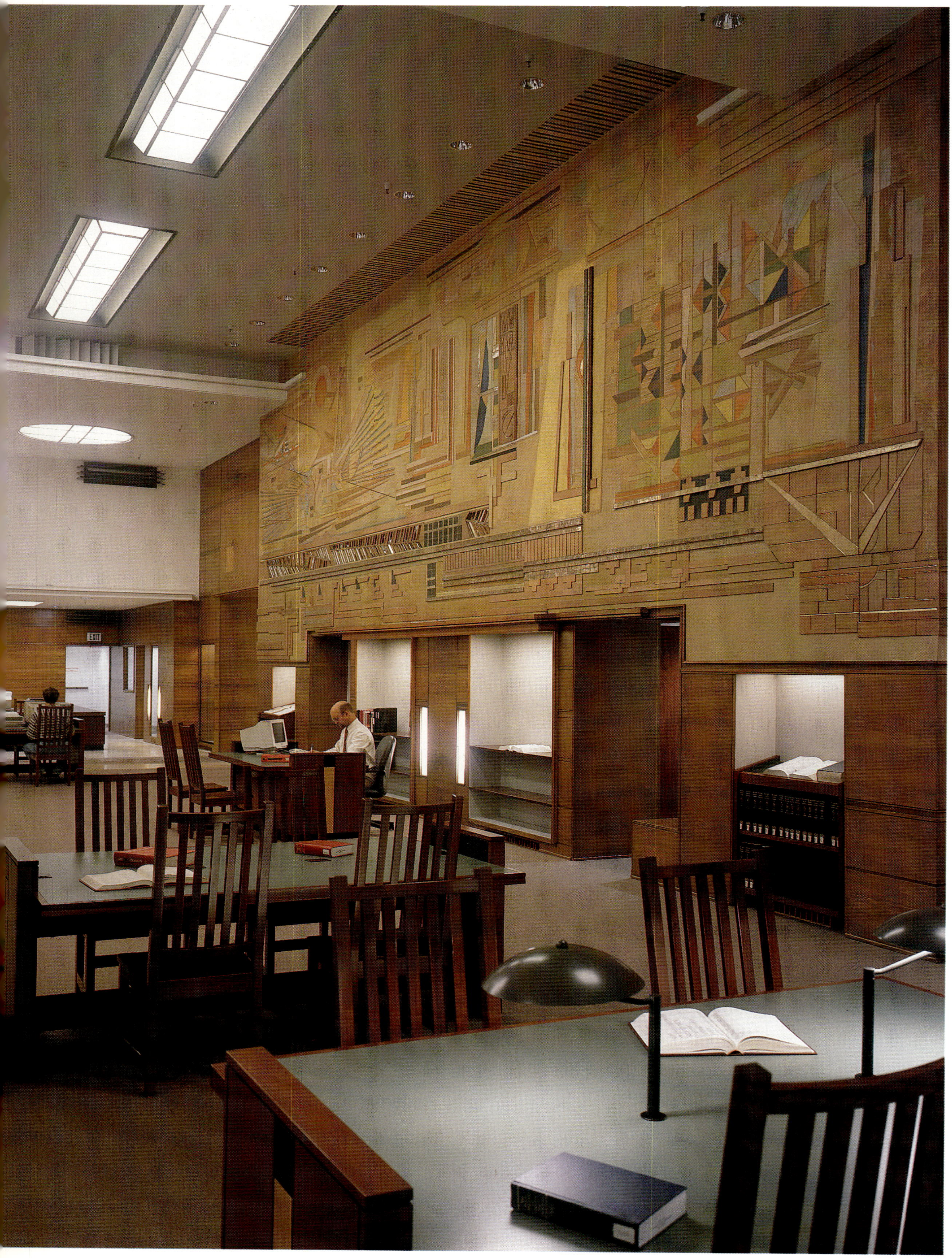

Opposite page, the reference desk and the "Spirit of Sports" mural. Above, the circulation desk.

84

Opposite page, the reading room and, below, the media room and computer classroom.

Details of the stack and carrels and of the reading tables.

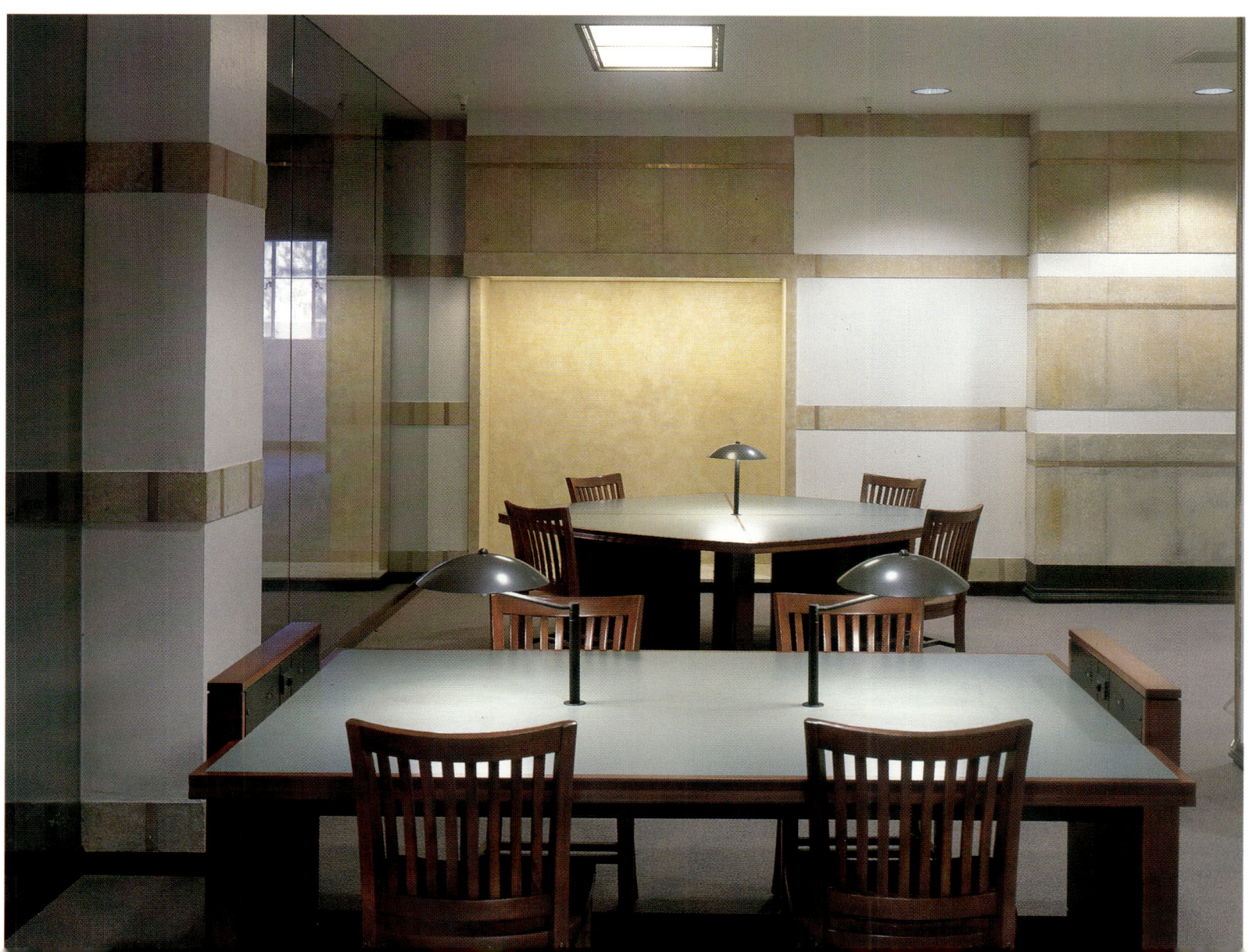

Views of the display cases and of the California Collection.

The reference collection.

The index table and clock wall.

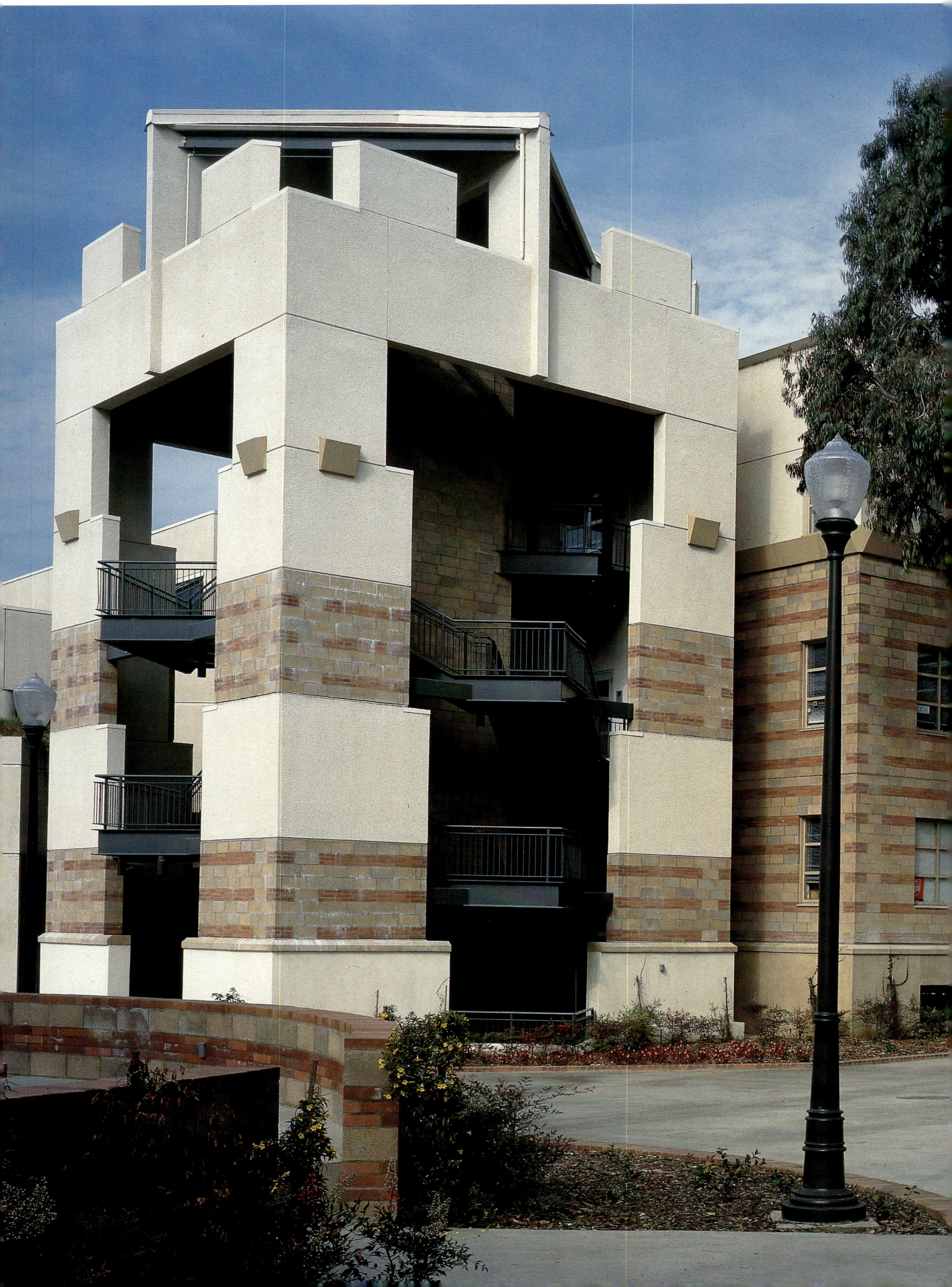

UCLA Wooden Center East and John Wooden Center Expansion

When the University of California at Los Angeles' Capital Programs Design retained Altoon + Porter Architects to expand the existing John Wooden Center and design the Wooden Center East, the UCLA campus was a study in assorted architectural styles. Built in three distinct epochs, the campus lacked the harmony and formal order intended by the original master planners. Altoon + Porter's challenge was to reclaim the legacy of the earliest buildings and set a pattern for future building that would honor the context of the university.

A survey of the campus revealed six buildings of the Epoch I master plan. Formal buildings, designed in a northern Italian Romanesque style, they were monumental in scale yet modified by delicate cloisters at their base. These inviting buildings with their intimate detail encouraged informal gatherings of students, thus reinforcing the sense of campus. Epoch II is marked by the post-World War II science buildings designed in an over-scaled, international style. In sharp contrast to the philosophy of the first generation, these buildings are anti-social in design. Finally, the coldly sculptural buildings of Epoch III are wedged uncomfortably between the buildings of the other epochs.

The original Wooden Center building was built during Epoch III, adjacent to an Epoch I landmark designed under the direction of George Kelham, the original master planner of the university. Due to its unfortunate siting, the building not only destroyed the gracious campus sensibility established by its neighbor, but did so at the critical junction of the school's major east-west internal axis and the north-south link to the adjoining commercial village.

In their design of Wooden Center East and the John Wooden Center expansion, Altoon + Porter reinstated the architectural value system of the original campus plan. The concept was to design a thin "sliver" building that would surround the Epoch III building with three new façades that reflect the aesthetic of its Romanesque revival neighbor and extends the Epoch I precinct through a greater portion of the campus. As importantly, this critical intersection would be redeemed by the legacy of the original campus plan.

Formal in its order and highly responsive to its context, Wooden Center East reinterprets the pattern mechanisms found in the adjacent Epoch I building through a contemporary architectural vocabulary. A mixture of brick and buff-colored concrete block, plaster, and terra cotta tiles, the façade of Wooden Center East responds to the primary, secondary, and tertiary orders of the Romanesque revival buildings. The design compliments the historic campus core, while the brickwork and plaster banding create a distinct new image for the building.

With the lessons learned from their retail experience, Altoon + Porter used simple architectural elements to connect the building to historic context and gave the campus an institutional building on a speculative budget. And the architects found a framework for future additions to the campus that recaptures the spirit of the original master plan and expands it throughout the campus.

Site plan.

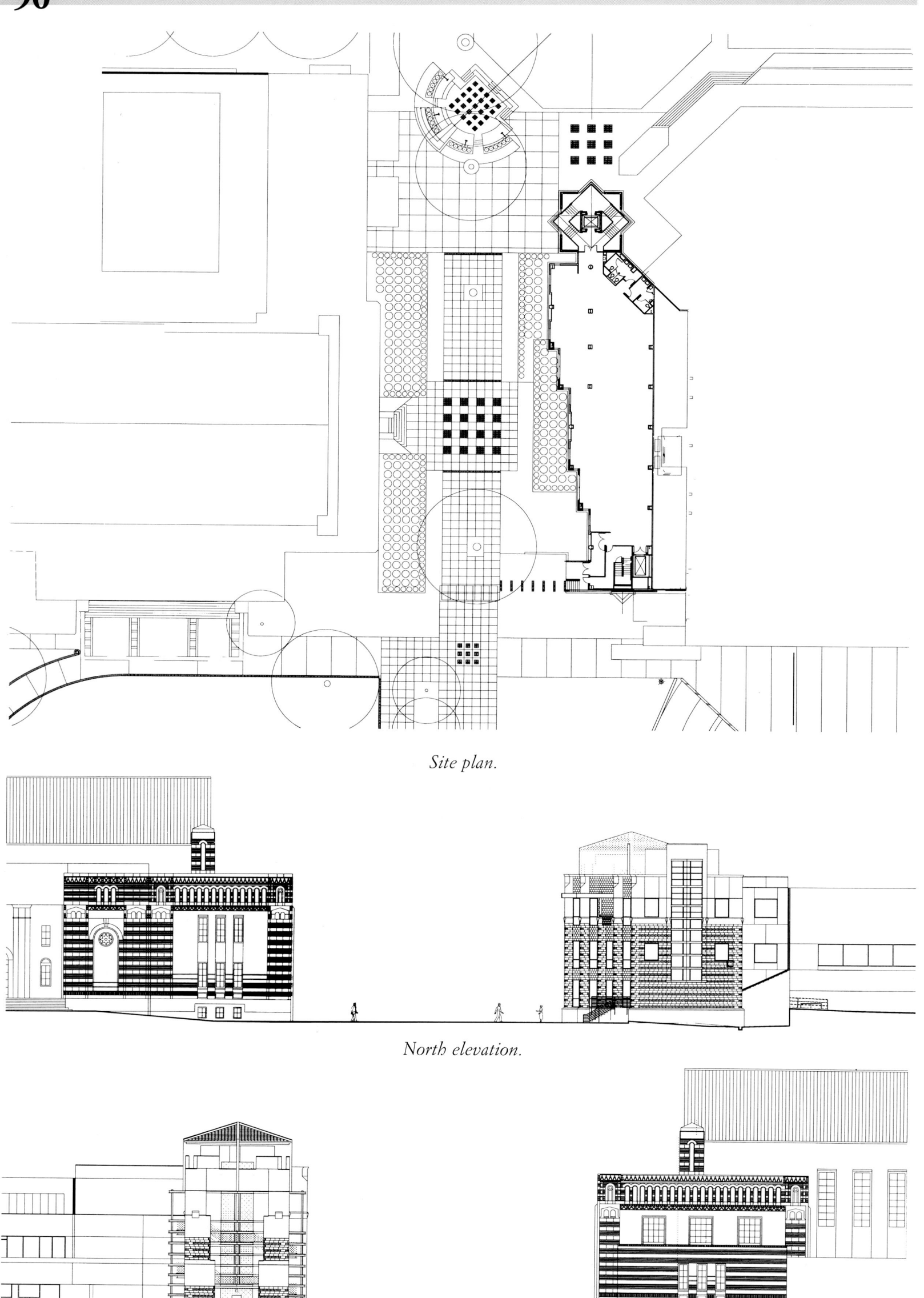

North elevation.

South elevation.

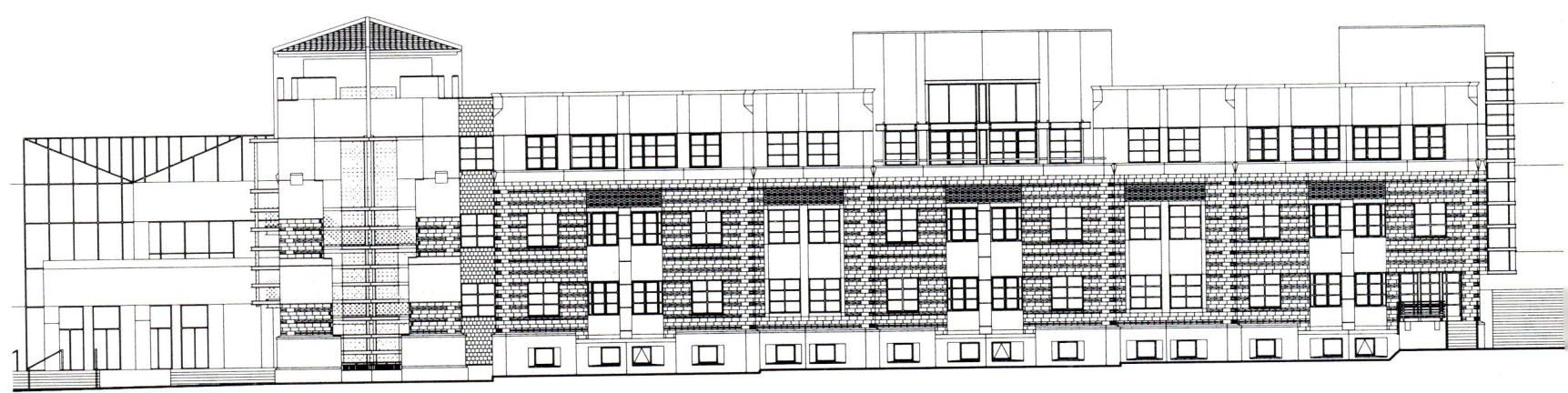

East elevation.

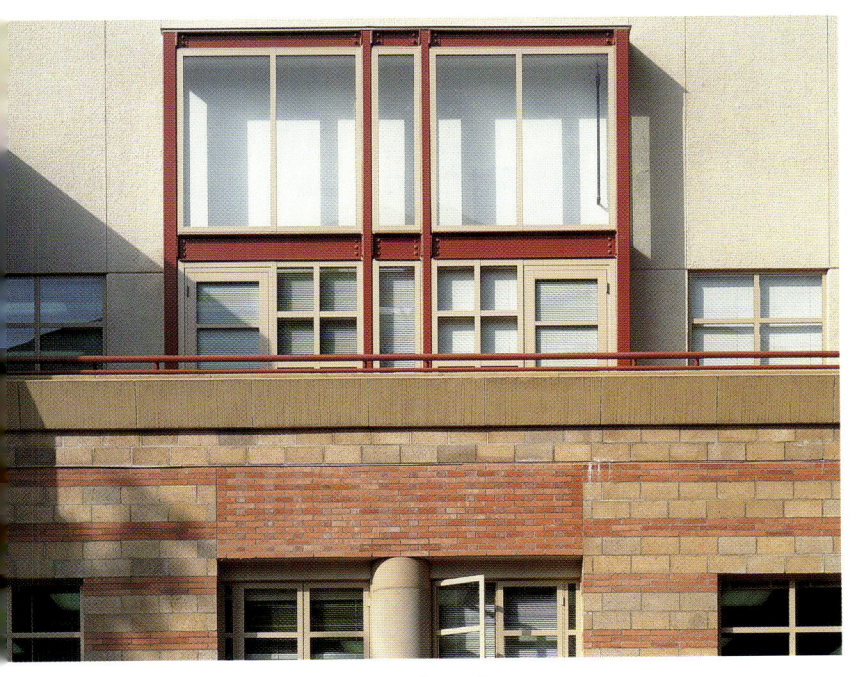

Terrace detail.

Window detail.

View of the east façade.

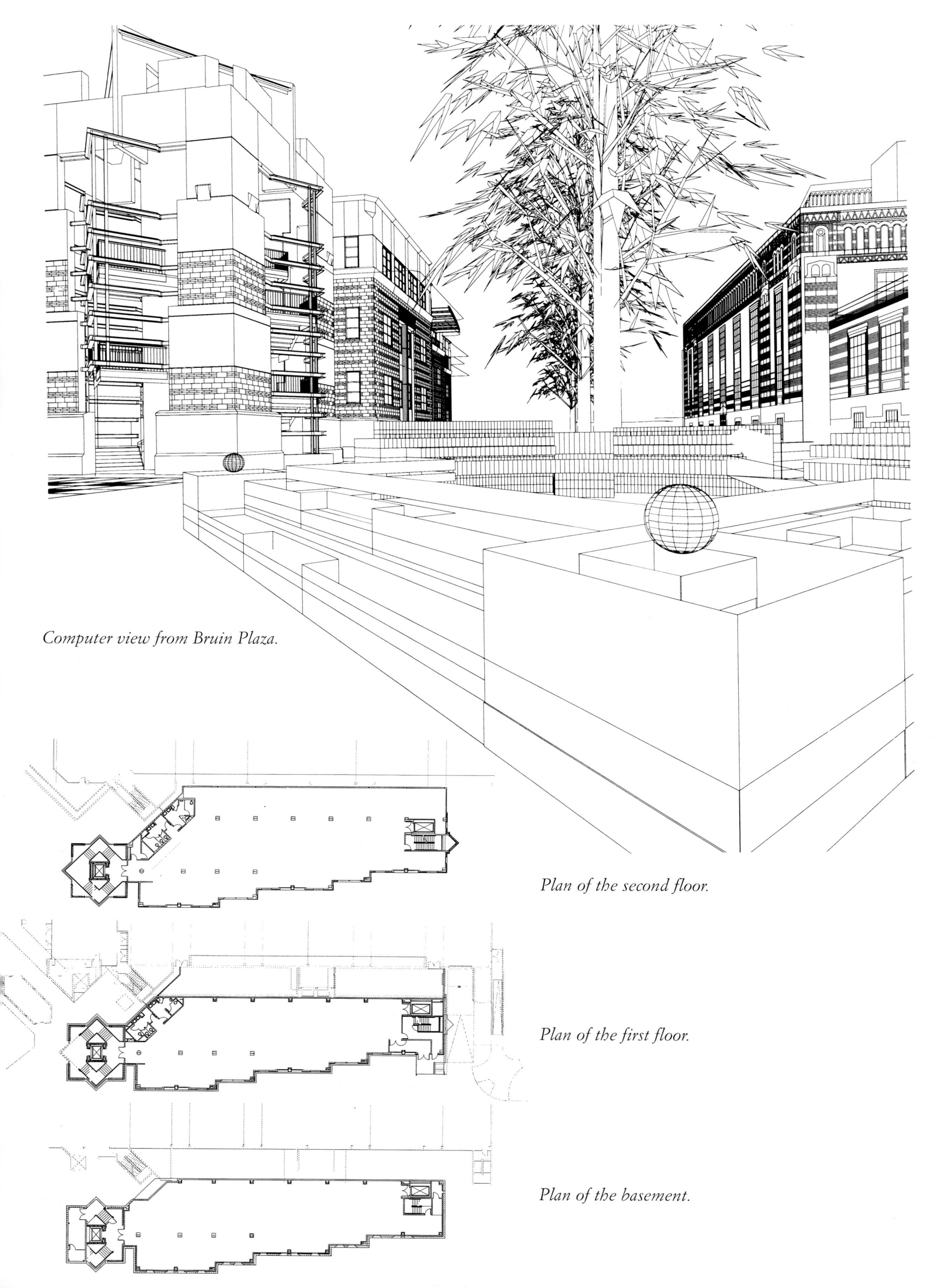

Computer view from Bruin Plaza.

Plan of the second floor.

Plan of the first floor.

Plan of the basement.

Computer view of Bruin walk. Below, detail of the glass tower.

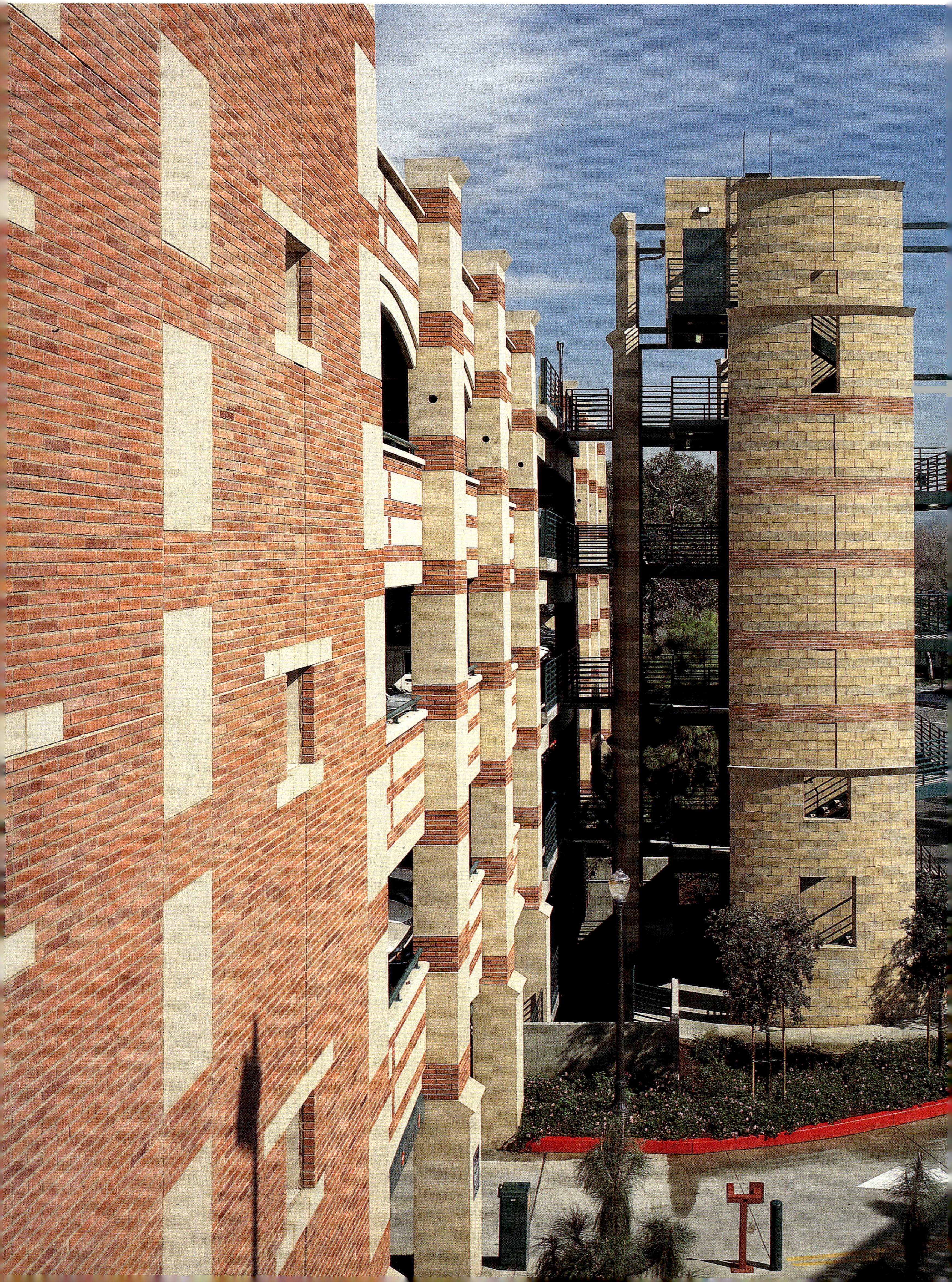

UCLA Parking Structure #3

The program for Parking Structure #3 called for the addition of 845 parking spaces to the existing seven-level garage. However, Altoon + Porter Architects understood that the commission was an opportunity to reconsider the context of the structure and complete the building. Located on a prominent corner of the UCLA campus, where the university faces the elegant neighborhoods of Bel Air and Holmby Hills, the parking structure posed an unusual problem of context. It was an industrial building on an institutional campus that formed part of a residential streetscape.

Altoon + Porter sought to integrate the building to the context in two ways. First, they pulled the vertical pedestrian circulation to the outside of the facility to create a tower. This element, extracted in plan from the balance of the building form, serves to convey a sense of arrival at the edge of the campus. Much like the campanile of the Italian city states, it creates a landmark boundary.

The second solution links the structure to the campus through the use of material and façade patterning that corresponds to the earlier campus buildings. A study in wallmaking, the parking structure now presents a sensitive, friendly face to the adjacent neighborhood, thus "healing" the street edge.

For Altoon + Porter Architects the project reinforced their aesthetic commitment to context both physical and historical – regardless of the building type.

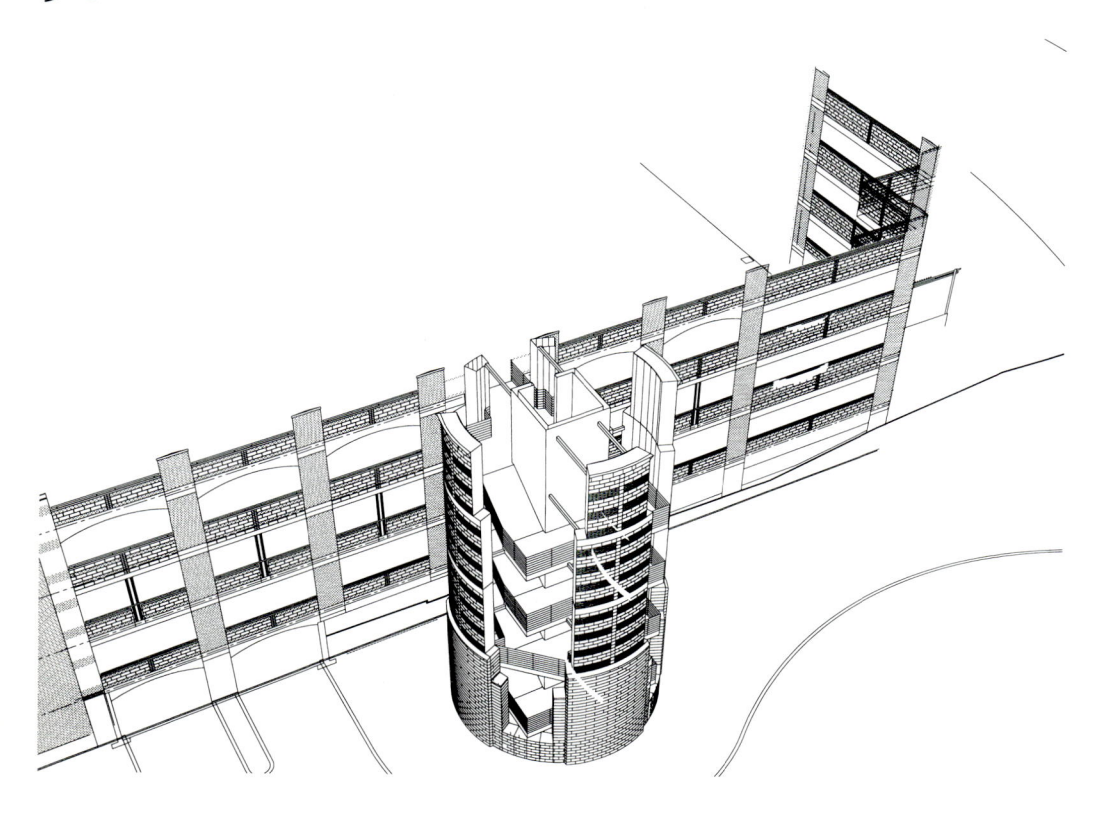

Computer massing study.

Tower detail.

97

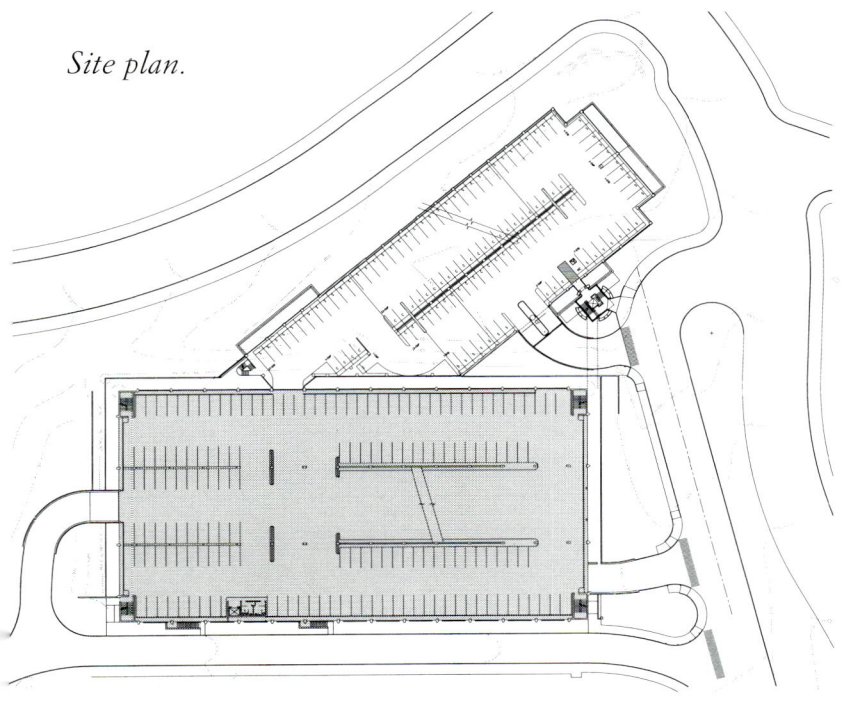

Site plan.

Façade detail.

View of the main façade.

The light fixture in the center court of Taman Anggrek Condominiums.

III. Trusting Intuition: An International Practice

By the mid-1990s, the superheated markets of the Asia Pacific created exceptional demand for architecture in every form – from retail complexes to high-rise residential towers to new transportation centers. Altoon + Porter's domestic profile, particularly in the commercial marketplace, captured the attentions of the first wave of Asian speculative developers. Having found their initial inspiration and confidence working in the multi-cultural mix of Southern California, the firm discovered the meaning of working with a variety of cultures on the other side of the globe.

Originally, clients came to the firm seeking a "copy" of the successful U.S. centers they had seen. But instead of designing an alien prototype, Altoon + Porter once again challenged its own aesthetic to create projects that are as indigenous in their own way as any of the projects of the firm. If the first transformation of the practice broke the mold and re-configured it in innovative ways, so this next evolution provided the opportunity for the firm to create new solutions based on an intuitive understanding of local culture and market needs.

On one hand, the projects are markedly modern solutions adapted to the demands of global corporations and mobile multi-national teams of architects, contractors, and financiers who are building tomorrow's buildings. On the other, they are local projects, constrained by climate, context, and culture. Altoon + Porter recognizes this dichotomy and has found design responses that capture the local in the abstract, working to bring the best of modern technological advances to bear without destroying the sense of place that makes a project part of its world.

Examples can be seen on projects at all scales, from a handrail that mirrors local plant life to paving patterns that are reminiscent of coral beds. Even the most Western of forms – the high-rise tower – reflects the local culture in a curtain wall that echoes the distinctive fabric patterns of the country.

But a project is more than details. The central building blocks of a development type can be broken down and reassembled in a fashion that is respectful of the new environment. Informed by their personal heritage, their formal training, and their success, the architects at Altoon + Porter understand that in this broad new global economy, intuition transcends rules.

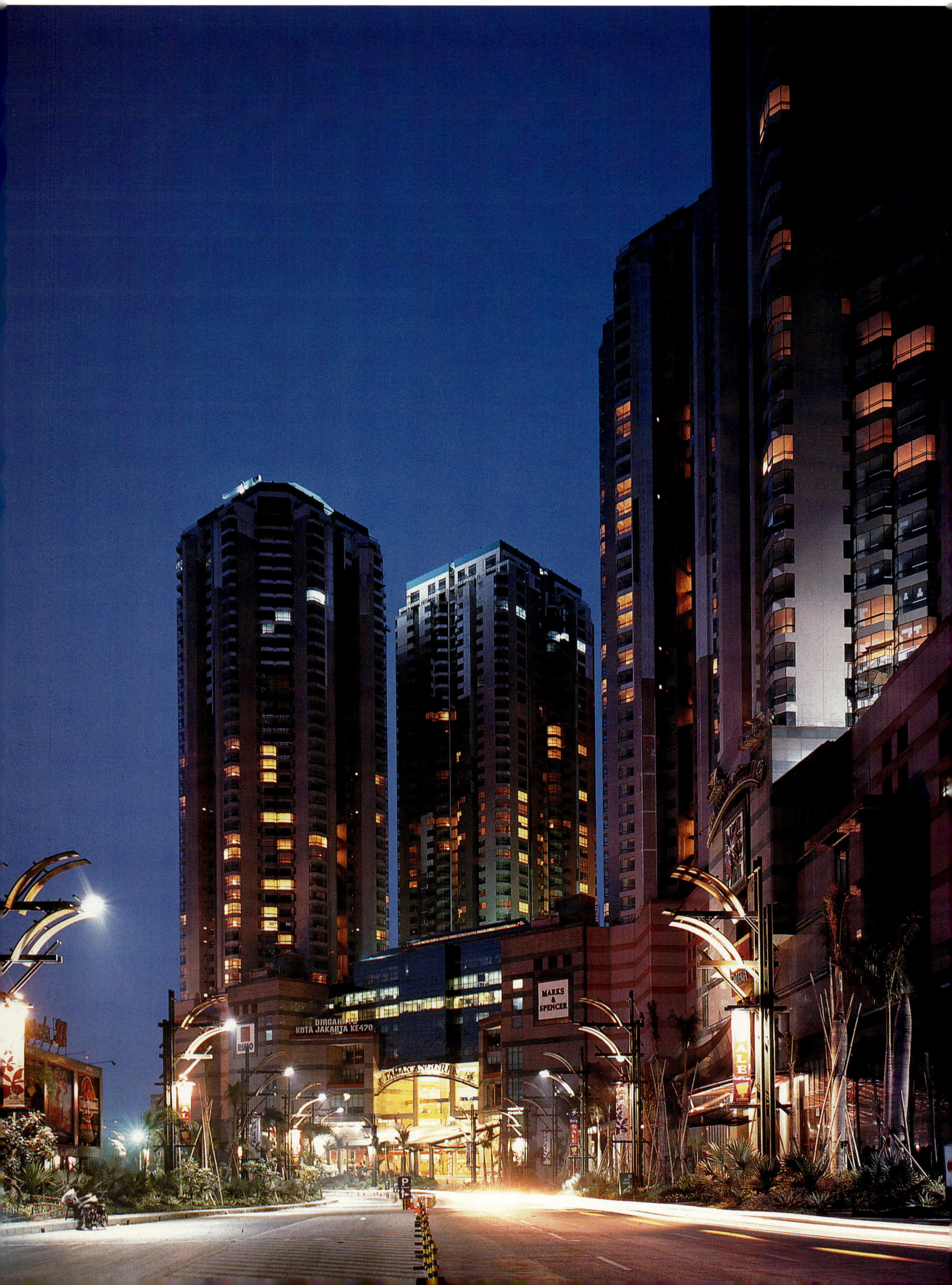
MARKS
&
SPENCER

Taman Anggrek Mall and Condominiums

Altoon + Porter was commissioned by one of the foremost development firms in Southeast Asia to design "a city within a city" that combines high-rise condominium units with a multi-level retail center. Identified as Southeast Asia's largest and most comprehensive retail/entertainment complex, Taman Anggrek demanded an innovative design solution that could meet Indonesia's thirst for a sophisticated retail experience without compromising the richness of its cultural heritage.

Named for the orchid gardens that once flourished on its site, the center is a melding of context-inspired design and state-of-the-art development. The Taman Anggrek Towers draw not only their name but their distinct form from these gardens. Altoon + Porter derived the floor plan of each residential tower from the image of the orchid. But the skin of the building borrows its design from tapis (the traditional fabric so closely identified with Indonesia) and wraps the building in the familiar rhythmic pattern.

Blunted angles soften the impact of the building's mass against the natural landscape while simultaneously making a dramatic and powerful statement. A porte-cochère entrance creates a grand sense of arrival for shoppers, and indigenous plants and cascading waterfalls grace the interior.

Taman Anggrek contains 1.5 million square feet of retail on six levels including a 1,200-seat food court and Southeast Asia's first ice-skating rink, as well as eight 36-story residential towers perched above the podium levels. Opening with 97 percent of the stores leased and all 2,950 condominium units pre-sold, the concept was well received by the market.

The center is broken down into shopping districts that create linked pockets of energy. This merchandising concept reduces the center's grand scale and keeps visitors from being overwhelmed by the mega-proportions. Beyond the 700 shops, the mall entices visitors with a variety of other retail attractions and entertainment destinations. The second level offers two automobile showrooms – modeled on the new generation of car boutiques in Japan. On the top two levels are the "energy floors" where shoppers discover food and entertainment in the form of an international standard ice-skating rink with a winterland annex featuring real snow, areas for virtual reality games, a 6-screen cineplex, and a disco. On the fifth floor are two food courts, one featuring specialties from around the world, and one serving as Indonesia's largest domestic food market.

Taman Anggrek is a lively, manageable shopping experience within a huge scale. The center provides modern, big-city amenities while remaining accessible to visitors. Although the retail concept is distinctly western, Altoon + Porter preserved the local flavor, proving that culturally sensitive projects can compete on the world stage.

The entrance and porte cochère. Opposite page, view of the center court and observation elevators.

103

View of center court.

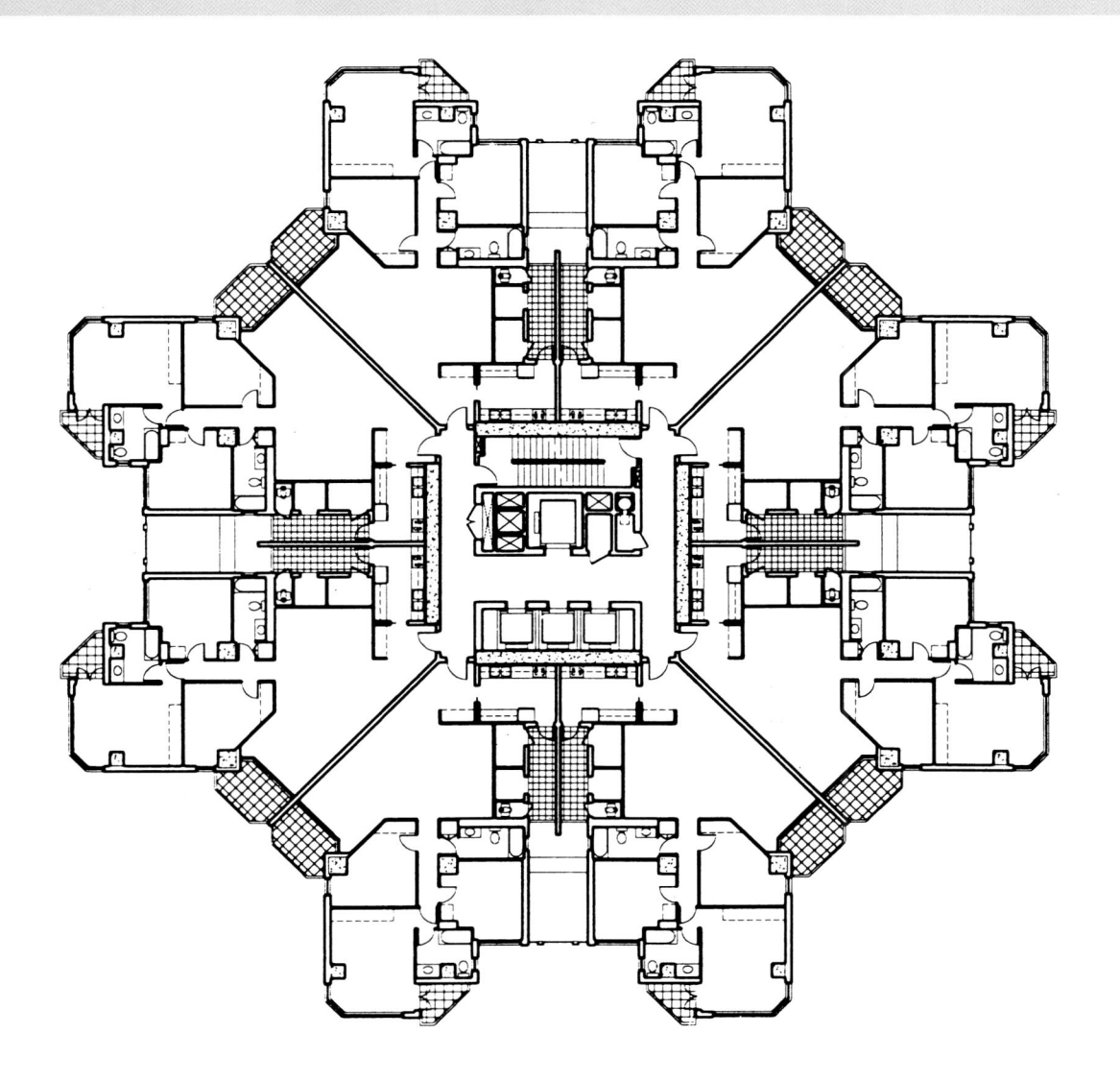

Plans of the tower.

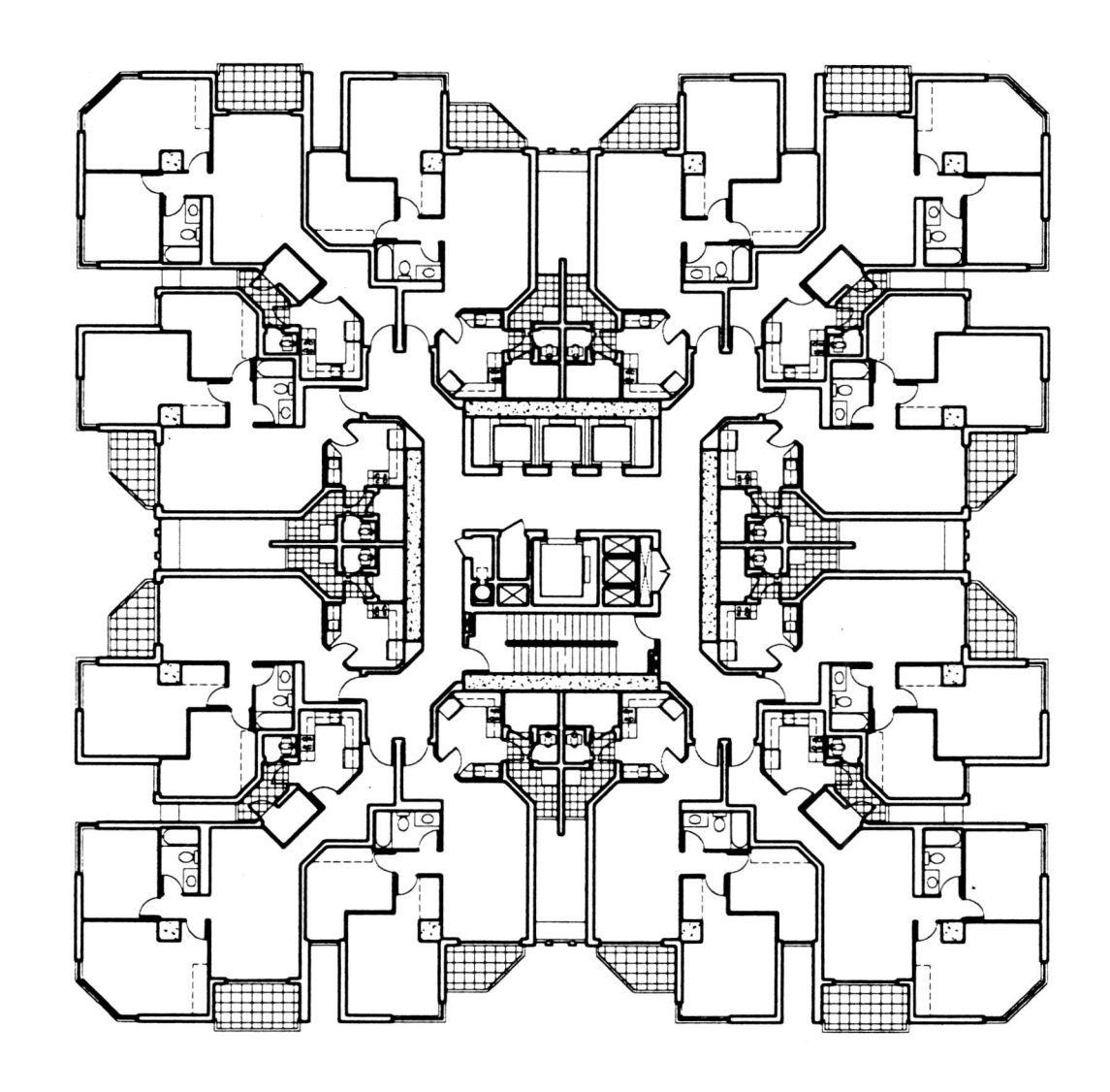

Indonesian Projects Master Planning and Conceptual Design

Altoon + Porter's Indonesian projects initially challenged the firm's long-held design beliefs. How would it be possible to create contexutally-sensitive projects in an environment that was rapidly transforming from the low-tech, small scale buildings of a Third World country to a sophisticated free-market economy housed in modern high-rise towers? In order to address the transitional nature of the context, the architects recognized that they were building a framework for future development. The planning and conceptual design for the three mixed-use complexes – the Jakarta Hotel and Shopping Center, Capitol Center, and Five Pillars – reflect the designers' understanding of the need to redefine context in light of impending changes.

The designs respond to the unique physical parameters of the specific sites yet the efforts share an approach that gives a formal order and iconic image to the developments. Moreover, each project considers the possibilities of future, adjacent development in such a way that the design of a complex is at once complete and the first phase of a larger vision of district.

Jakarta Hotel and Shopping Center

Altoon + Porter Architects was commissioned to design a new hotel that would combine luxury accommodations with upscale retail. The triangular, 1.4-hectare site at the key intersection of two major roadways is an excellent location, close to the central business district. Located adjacent to the Garuda, a national landmark sculpture, the project is destined to become a landmark in its own right.

Altoon + Porter met the challenges of the site with a design that borrows its metaphor of flight from the Garuda. Like the statue, the building boldly projects its face toward the arrival route from the international airport while its wings are pulled back sheltering the retail component that faces the city of Jakarta.

With a 10-meter setback from the boundary line along the southerly airport road, and an eight-meter setback along the two other roads, the building mass could not encroach into the setback, however driving ramps and porte-cochère canopies were permissible. Below grade construction could encroach up to three meters from the boundary line.

The solution is a retail podium supporting the five-star hotel which will include a grand department store, a secondary department store, a supermarket, a six-screen cinema, retail shops, restaurants, and a food court in 35,000-45,000 square meters. On top of this shopping complex, a 400-room hotel with a 24-hour restaurant, a bar, a sub-dividable conference room, a business center, and administration, laundry, kitchen, and service facilities will be built. Other amenities will include a rooftop pool, a fitness center, and a garden. Parking for the building will be located on three, subterranean levels along with servicing for the complex. Approximately 1,350-1,400 spaces have been planned.

The shopping center will be directly accessible from the street and the parking structure. The parking will ramp up to a porte-cochère overlooking a terraced fountain. An elevator from the third floor will take guests up to a fifth-floor lobby for check-in. There will also be a grand staircase extending from the third floor to the fifth.

Longitudinal section.

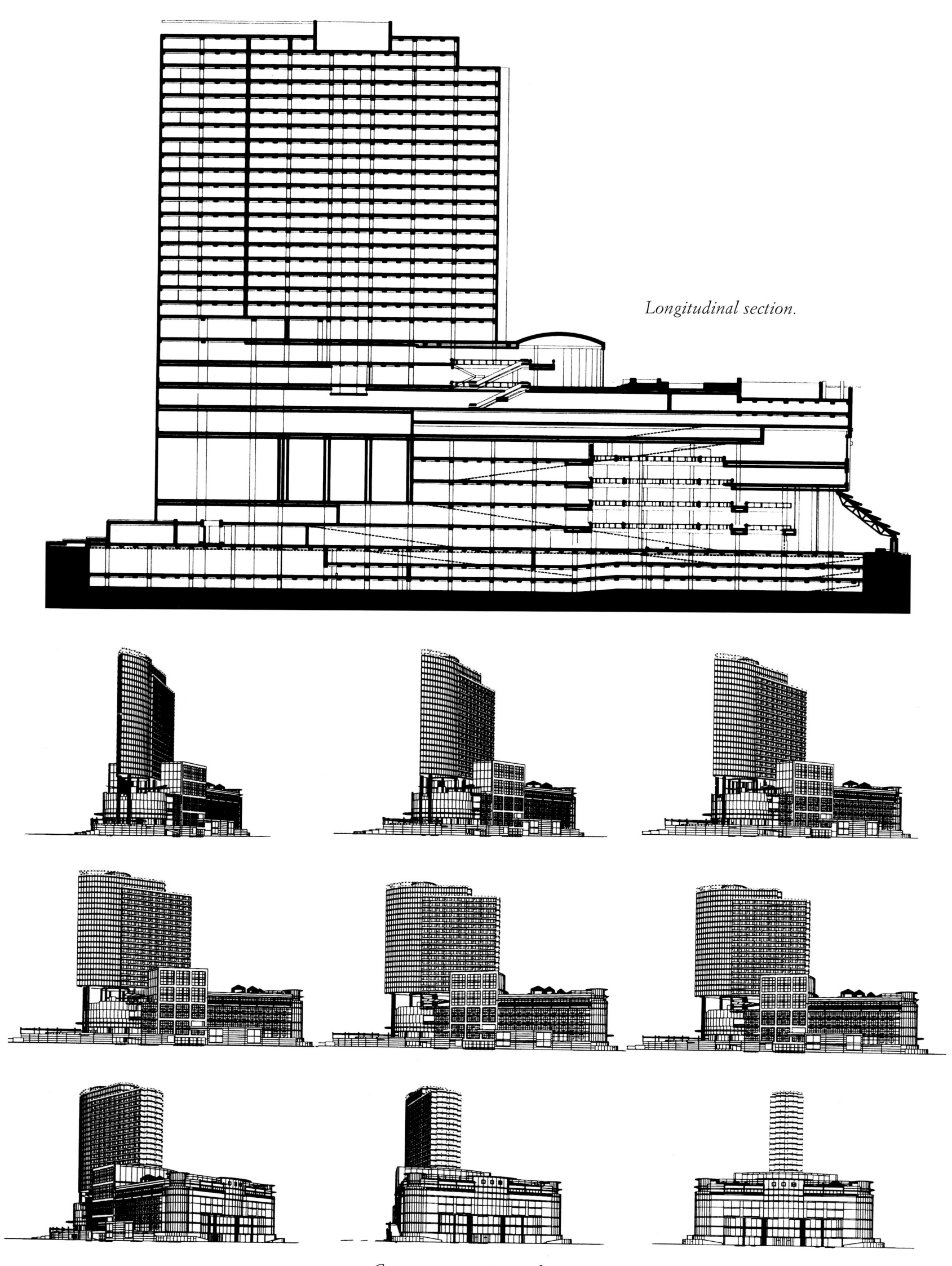

Computer massing studies.

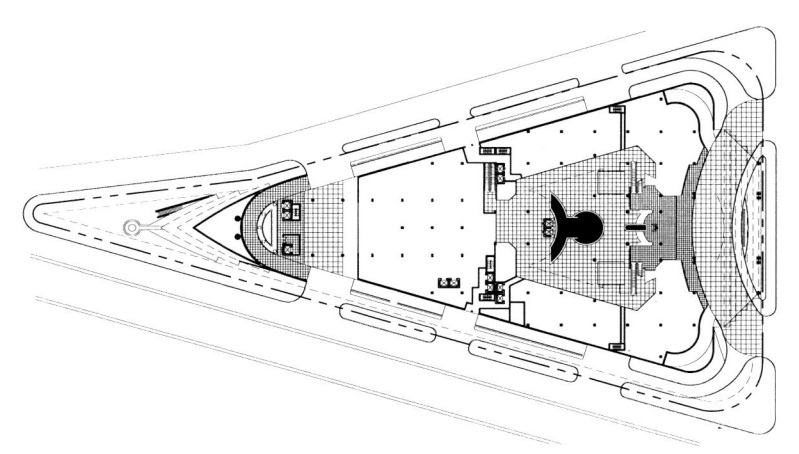

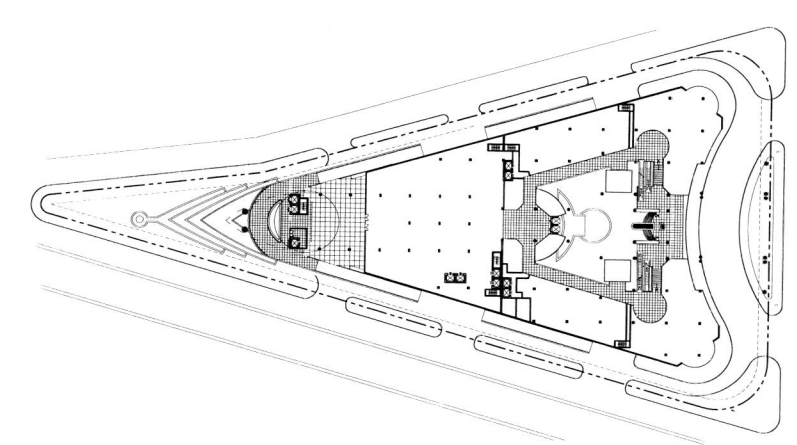

Plan of the sixth floor.

Plan of the fifth floor.

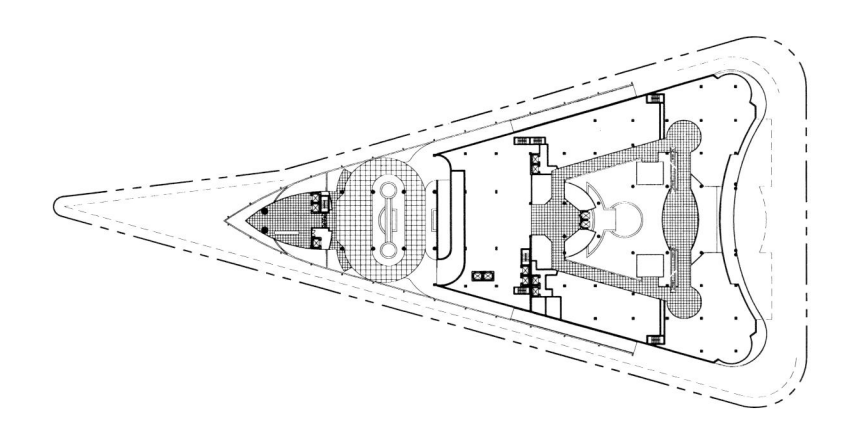

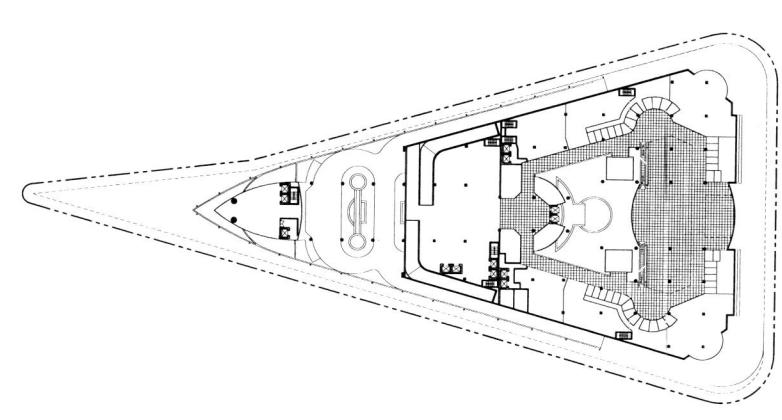

Plan of the fourth floor.

Plan of the third floor.

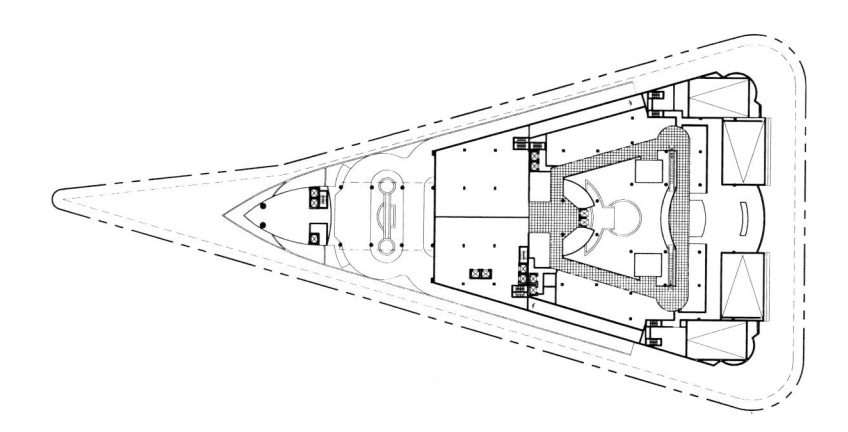

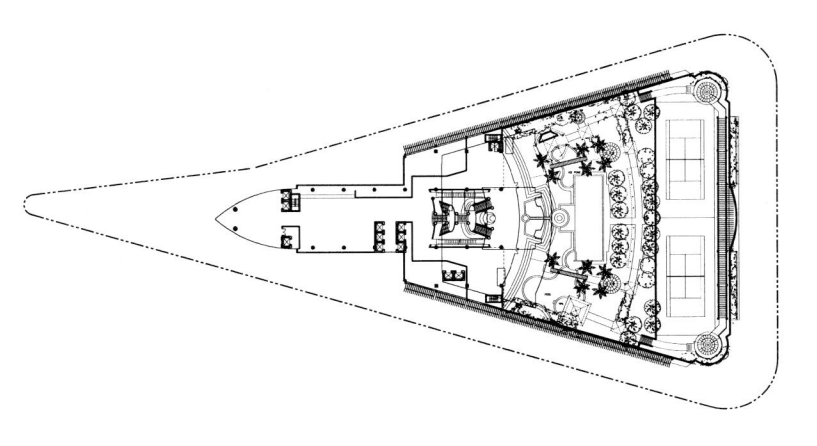

Plan of the second floor.

Plan of the first floor.

Perspective view.

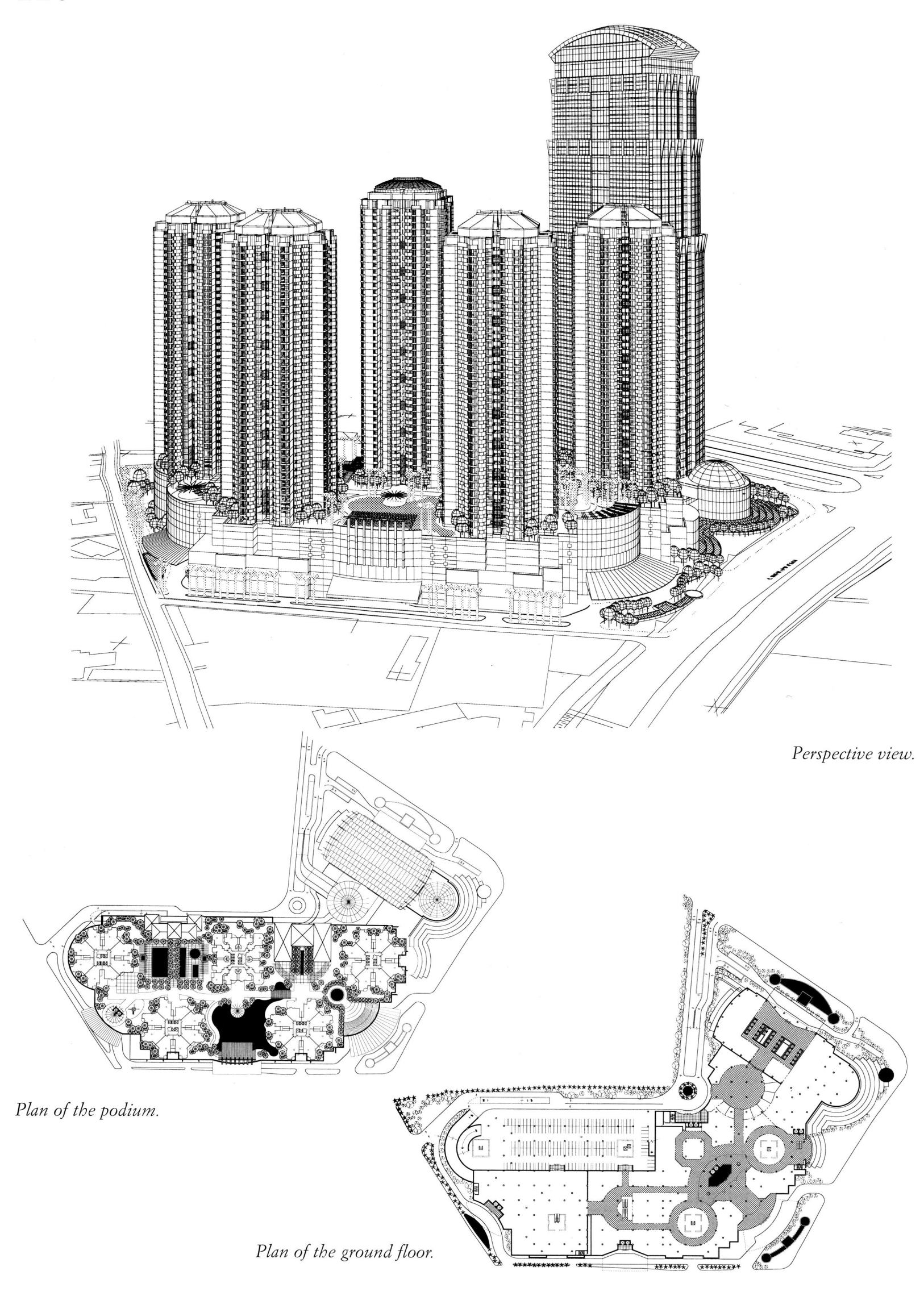

Plan of the podium.

Plan of the ground floor.

Capitol Center

Capitol Center, a sophisticated, multi-use complex, will be located in the Golden Triangle, an area containing some of the most expensive real estate in central Jakarta. Capitol Center's program called for prime office space in a new 60-story tower, five luxury highrise apartment buildings, a three-story retail center, and four levels of parking for over 5,500 cars designed to cater to businesses, shoppers, and residents alike.

The design signals the formal order of the complex. A glazed corner element marks the entrance to the retail center which, with the parking area, will be located in the base of the complex. The office tower and residential buildings rest on top of this base. Organized around a three-story atrium, the center will contain two major department stores and small retail boutiques. Two glass elevators provide circulation and serve as moving observation decks.

The retail base acts as a podium that will lift the office tower and residential buildings above the city. The five residential buildings are organized around a plaza level located just above the retail center. Suspended over this base, the highrise buildings will have an innovative structural system generated by the parking grid. Additional support for the buildings will be provided by the vertical circulation cores that contain elevators and escalators.

Located 100 feet above the ground, the plaza level will contain raised private gardens with lush plantings, pools, lagoons, an orchid house, and trellises that create shaded paths for passive recreation. The plaza level also offers residents opportunities for active recreation with a health club, tennis courts, a spa, a children's play area, an Olympic-sized pool, and a children's wading pool.

The residential towers will be situated at the periphery of the site to maximize views of the surrounding area. Four of the towers are designed in an octagonal shape with eight residential units per floor. These surround a slightly taller, square tower with 12 units on each level. Together, the five residential towers contain 1,683 luxury apartments including top-floor penthouses.

Although integrated into the complex, the office tower is set apart from the residential buildings. Its drop-off area is distinguished by a landscaped court and an entrance canopy. The speculative office spaces are designed to American standards with open floor plans serviced by three banks of elevators. Clad in glass with granite column covers, the office tower will have a distinctive rectangular shape with curved ends. As it rises over the housing towers and the plaza, the tower leans back to provide panoramic views of the surrounding city.

112

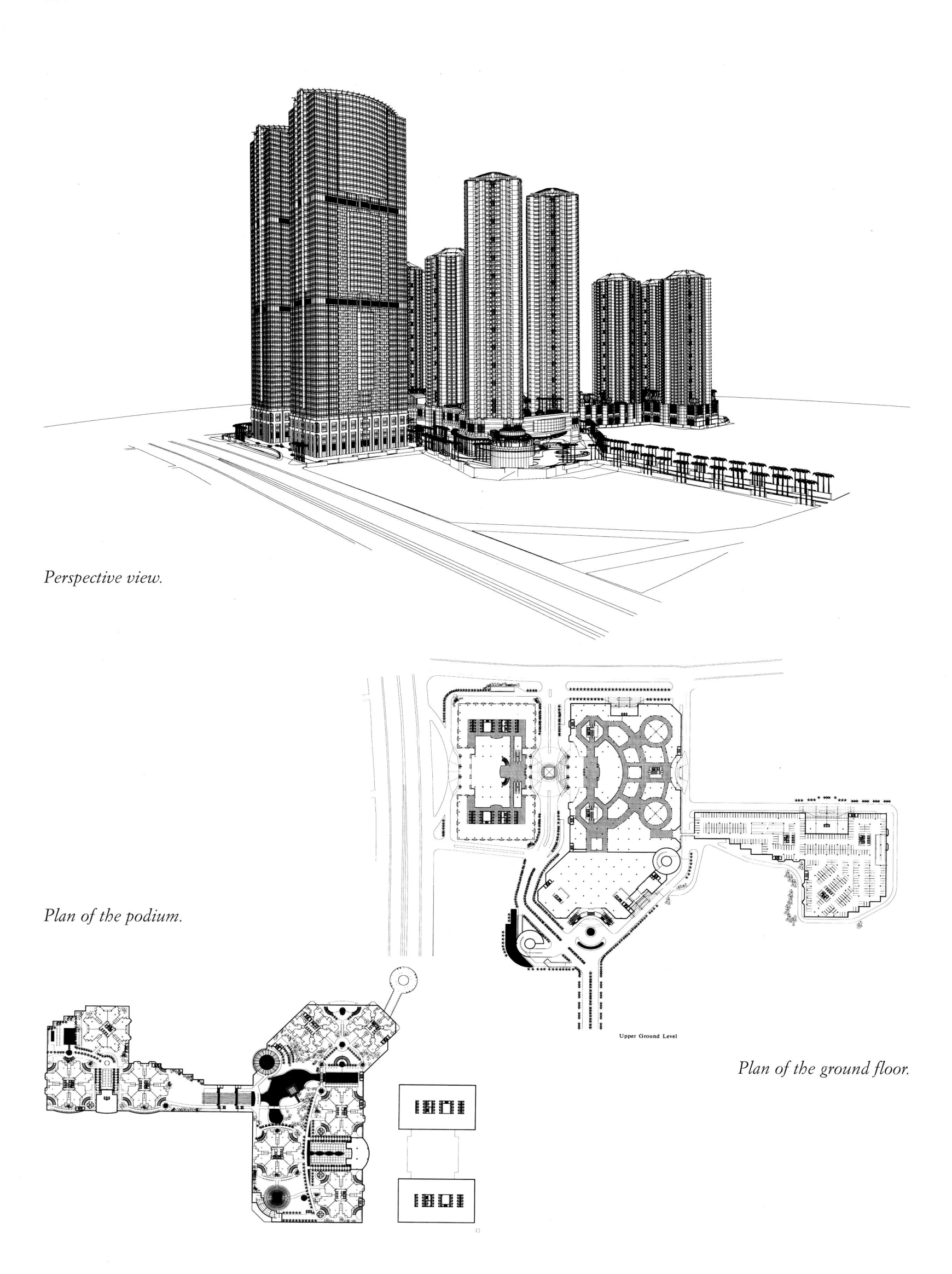

Perspective view.

Plan of the podium.

Upper Ground Level

Plan of the ground floor.

Five Pillars

Located along an important corridor between downtown Jakarta and the airport, the Five Pillars complex, which contains two office towers, eight residential towers with gardens, a retail center, and parking, is a new center for business, residence, and regional shopping.

The complex establishes an armature for future development growth with a project whose order is easily understood. The office towers are the tallest buildings and the most visible. The strong rectilinear forms will have glass curtain walls with stainless steel detailing and a cantilevered, elliptical form at the top which gives the towers a distinct character. The base of the towers contains commercial facilities which connect the office buildings to the adjacent housing towers.

Outfitted in stone, the residential base is a sign of permanence and solidity next to the glass façades of the office towers. The residential buildings are placed on two parts of the site. The buildings are located across from the office towers and includes a regional shopping center at the base. Arranged around a central atrium, the complex contains a major department store, a food court, a supermarket, and upscale retail as well as home-related stores and services to accommodate the needs of daily life.

Above this base, three octagonal-shaped buildings are arranged symmetrically facing the office towers, and two square towers face a local access road. The buildings contain light and ventilation zones carved into the façades, almost to the core, that allow air to circulate throughout the apartments. Three additional residential buildings are located at a slightly lower grade above a parking deck at the far end of the site.

The two residential areas are connected by a continuous garden level above the base with a bridge spanning the two parts of the site. The gardens include meandering and formal paths, water features including a lagoon and a waterfall, tea houses, and grass lawns. A range of lush plants and terrain represents the rich variety of the Indonesian landscape. Other amenities include a health club, tennis courts, swimming pools, and play areas.

114

Warringah Mall

It was not only the opportunity to work in Australia, the "Land Down Under," that caused Altoon + Porter Architects to turn the rules of retail design upside down. The firm's aesthetic had evolved. Now, in place of refined details and formal elements that marked the firm's earlier projects is an unexpected iconography. Still highly conscious of locale and culture, Altoon + Porter's new design demonstrates an ability to abstract the essence of context in much the same way that they transformed the original idea of a "kit of parts" into a rich, multifaceted, aesthetic language. The renovation and expansion of Warringah Mall is a striking example.

Sited on 16-hectares in a northern suburb of Sydney, Warringah Mall had a friendly, beach-side ambiance. But the disjointed layout, the result of decades of additions with numerous designers, robbed the center of synergy. Altoon + Porter was engaged to bring a visual clarity to the center that would create a sense of place and civic pride. Furthermore, the project was to be expanded with the addition of two new wings.

The architects' trademark study of contextual issues revealed the confluence of three separate ecological zones, all within the space of 1,000 yards surrounding Warringah Mall. From hills to valleys to sea, the scenery was as incongruous as the project itself. The buildings ranged from one totally enclosed wing to another that was semi-enclosed to yet another that was completely open air. This guided the architects to join the structures in ways that would be easily navigable and conceptually clear.

To create a distinctive destination, the architects embraced the diversity of the site and structure, isolating and celebrating individual elements of architecture and linking them together. The new design was open enough to reveal the richness of the flora and fauna of the Peninsula, yet structured enough to give order to the project's circulation pattern.

Taking advantage of the benign climate, the designers removed the roof to expose the retail levels to light and air. Abstractions of architectural icons from Sydney's beaches and deserts further integrated the mall with its environment. A series of indoor-outdoor shopping "neighborhoods," reflecting the casual lifestyle of the Northern Beaches, are linked to the new center court with glass-covered spines. These spines allow the shopper to move from one neighborhood to another without losing the strong sense of place.

Altoon + Porter responded to the client's desire for a civic component with an inviting open-air court at the center of the project. Maintaining the balance between a sense of relatedness and the diversity of the shops was critical – the new design added 133 tenant spaces along the arcades, complimenting the 140 existing retail units. All the glass-covered spines lead back toward the ivy-covered trellises that edge the perimeter of the center courtyard. This focuses the energy of the project and connects each of the separate neighborhood shopping districts. As the spines link the spaces, the bold iconography of elements connects the theme. Landscape featuring gardens, fountains, seating areas, and public art reinforce the design.

For the client, the revitalized Warringah Mall provides both a spirited celebration of the Northern Beaches and a retail destination of international caliber. For Altoon + Porter, the project provided the opportunity to push the retail prototype and their own design aesthetic to a new level.

View of the grand stair.

Detail of the exterior texture.

View of the atrium.

Detail of the pergola, below, the trellis and clerestory.

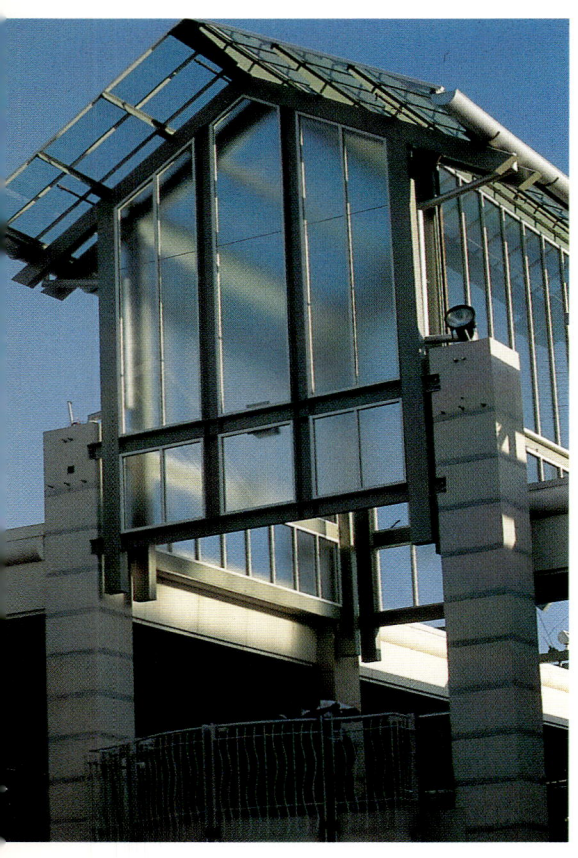

Details of the portal, the trellis and canopy, and of the native sandstone. Below, perspective view of the galleria.

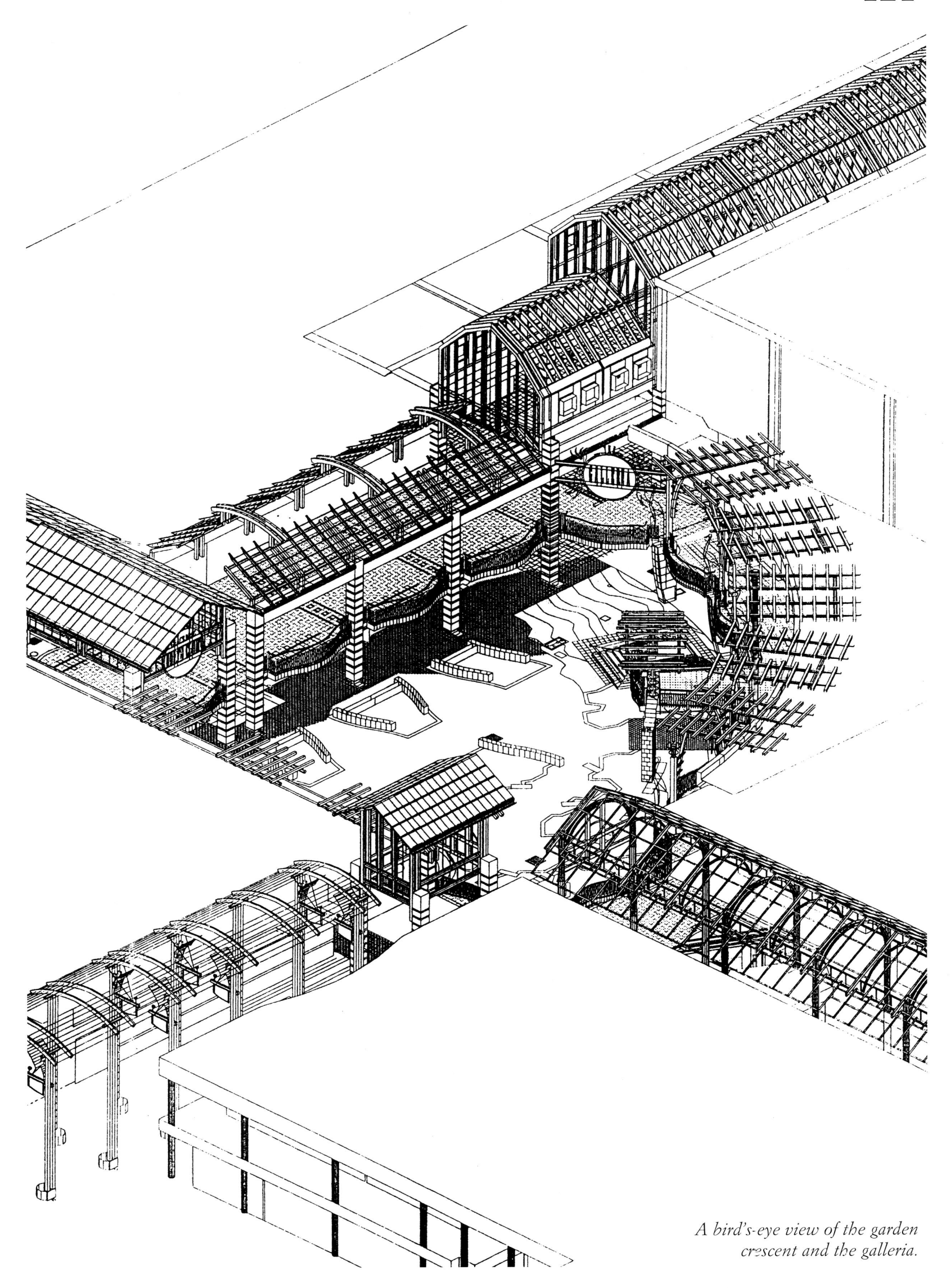

A bird's-eye view of the garden crescent and the galleria.

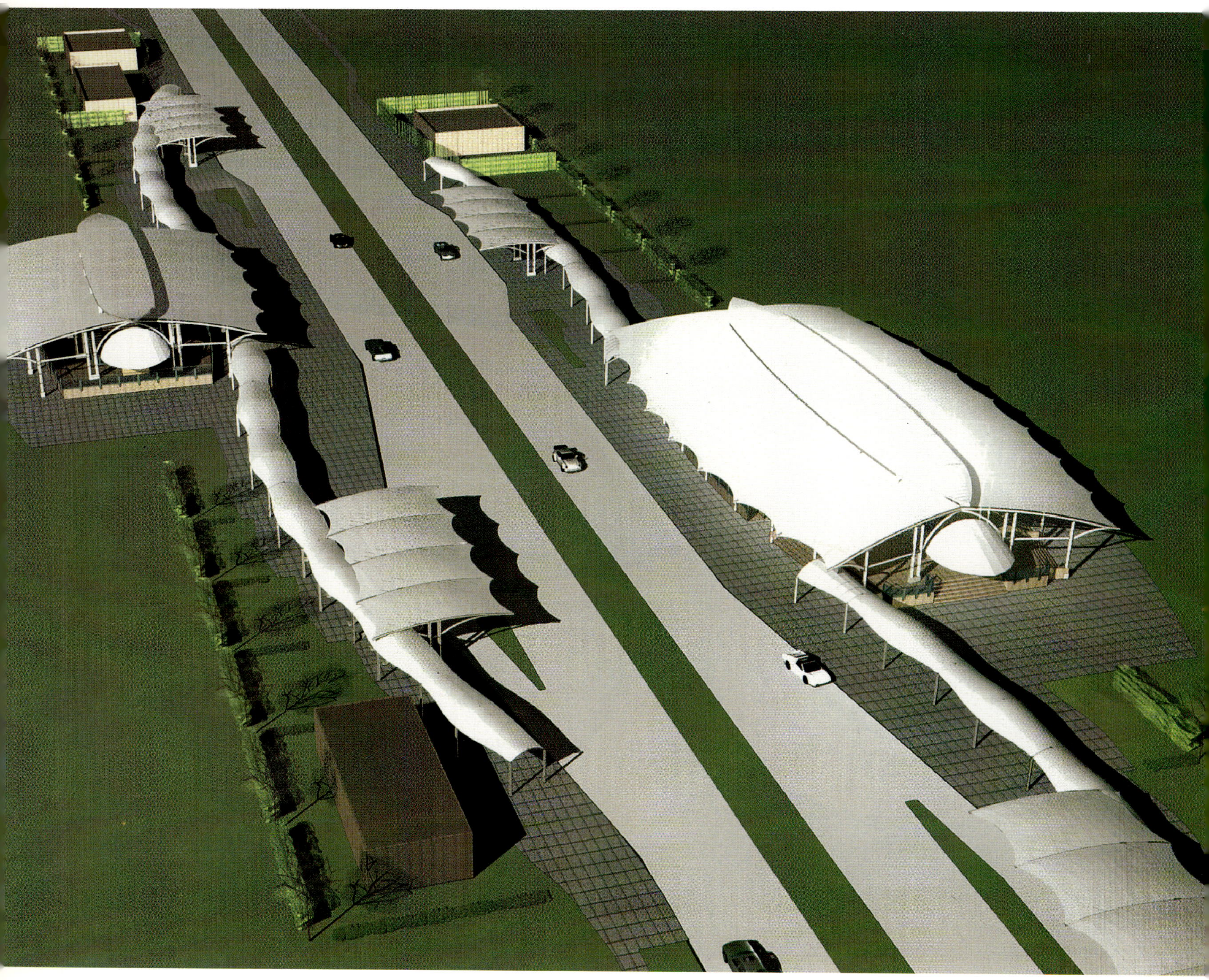

Buangkok and Sengkang Transit Stations

Although Altoon + Porter Architects had designed transit-oriented retail before, the assignment to do a purely transportation infrastructure project presented an opportunity to take the lessons of public placemaking learned in the commercial arena and apply them to a new building type. At the same time, the commission provided the firm with a cultural lesson on life in the Asia Pacific that would inform other projects as Altoon + Porter continues to serve a growing client base in the region.

The firm was commissioned to design two of the twelve new stations along Singapore's Northeast Line Expansion. The project, an important marker in the growth of the tiny, but powerful, island republic, embodies Singapore's commitment to world-class transportation infrastructure. While both stations enjoy the same benign climate and geography, each had a distinctly different set of design criteria. Buangkok Station is in a decidedly suburban setting; Sengkang Station is in an urban precinct.

Part of Singapore's pursuit of an active civil defense program, Buangkok Station is built below grade. As a component of this program, there is no permanent physical or visual connection to the station's interior from outside the station. The station entrances straddle the major roadway that runs above. They lead to the station platform at the lower level using a subterranean tunnel that serves even non-transit users who need to cross the large thoroughfare. Sinewy covered linkways flank the interior and are arranged to visually gather the various points along the roadway into a single space, helping to clearly distinguish the station entry from the other, above-ground elements.

Since almost no natural light penetrates the platform level, the use of artificial lighting is critical to Singapore's tradition of providing secure, comfortable, and clean transit. The sense of connection is also achieved through the use of patterns, materials, and layout that mirror the surface environment.

The more urban Sengkang Station stands at the center of a four-block square with a mix of uses ranging from commercial office and retail to residential. Unlike Buangkok, Sengkang Station is at the heart of a busy transportation junction adjacent to a bus depot and is situated beneath the above-ground light rail system.

Clarity of organization is paramount to the design of Sengkang Station and simplicity reinforces the recognition of pathways and destinations. Located within a complex of varying uses, the station is essentially "landlocked." The design solution compensates with an overhead, glass-enclosed oval that brings natural light from the roof-level light rail station to the mezzanine and platform levels. Elevators are strategically placed to enhance passenger flow and preserve the station's open spaces which allow light to move from the higher levels to the lower ones. This flow of light is critical as it creates a visual connection with the sky unlike any subway station in the world.

For all the distinctive differences between the design for Sengkang and Buangkok Stations, there are similarities. Specifically, a fabric treatment used successfully in several commercial designs done by the firm was introduced in the Singapore stations. The use of fabric was unprecedented in Singapore, but once Singapore Transit Authority officials recognized the effectiveness of the solution both as image and protection, they were excited by the materials.

At Buangkok, the Teflon-coated fabric covers the above-ground accesses, including the walkways and entrances to the station, while at Sengkang, both entrances and bridges were covered with the fabric. The material is ideally suited to Singapore's climate. It provides visual protection from the sun's intensity and ultraviolet light, and it protects waiting transit users from the brief but sudden tropical showers known to occur in the region.

At night, the tenting effect of the fabric becomes visible from afar. Because of this, the stations become beacons – distinguished landmarks against the skyline. The tenting done for these stations intentionally avoids an expo-like appearance. Eschewing the exaggerated look associated with the use of this material, the tenting for the stations has a simple and direct sensibility. It suggests the permanence and stability of a public space rather than the flexibility and transience of a fair.

Sengkang Station was designed to enhance its proximity to other services and transport connections. Buangkok Station was designed to mitigate the lack of natural light and overcome the low ceilings necessitated by civil defense parameters. These constraints provided an opportunity for Altoon + Porter to break with conventions and explore new applications for their aesthetic vocabulary.

Top, view of the covered walkways.
Above, view under the station
entrance canopy.

Study for the entrance canopy.

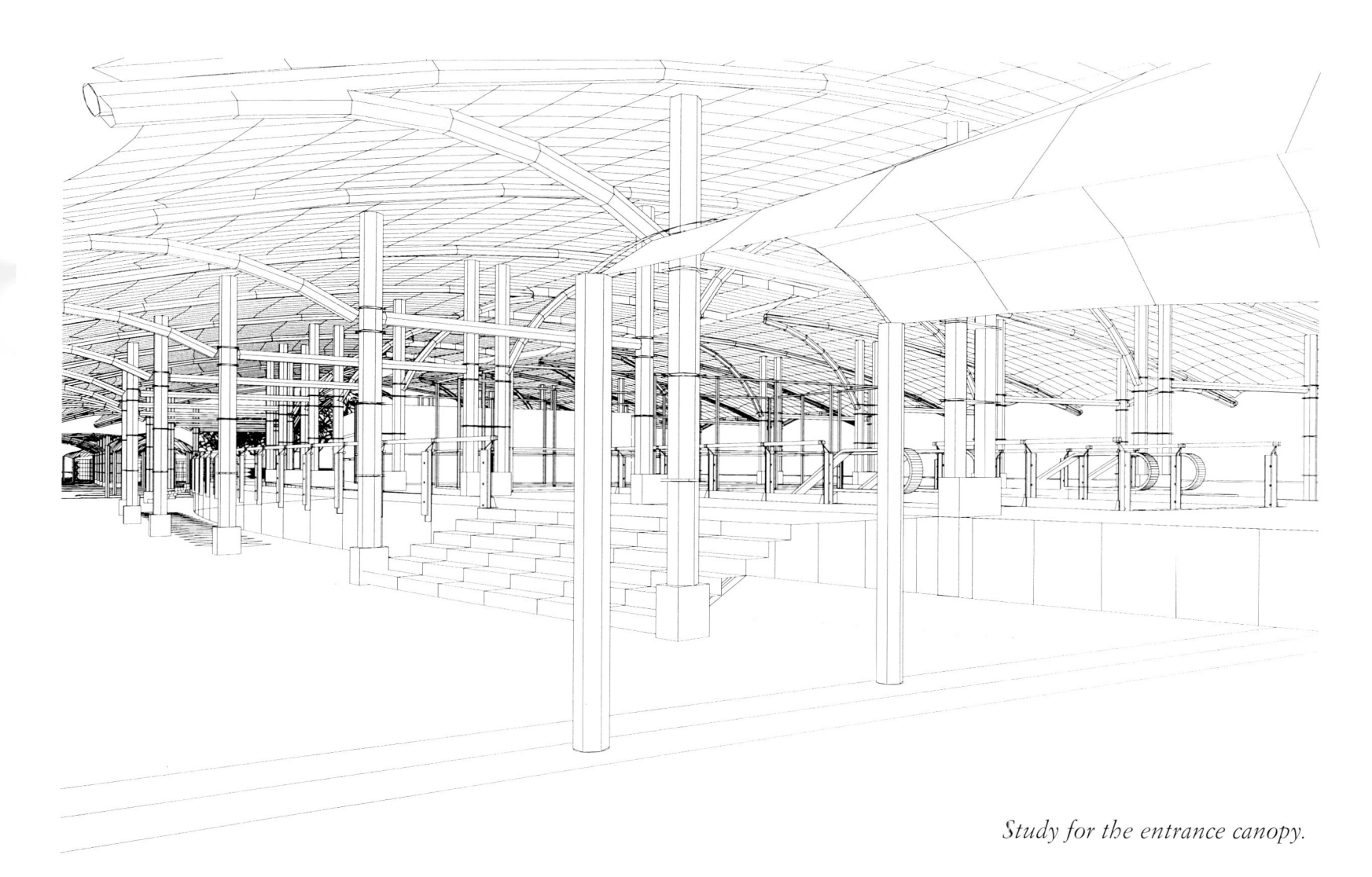

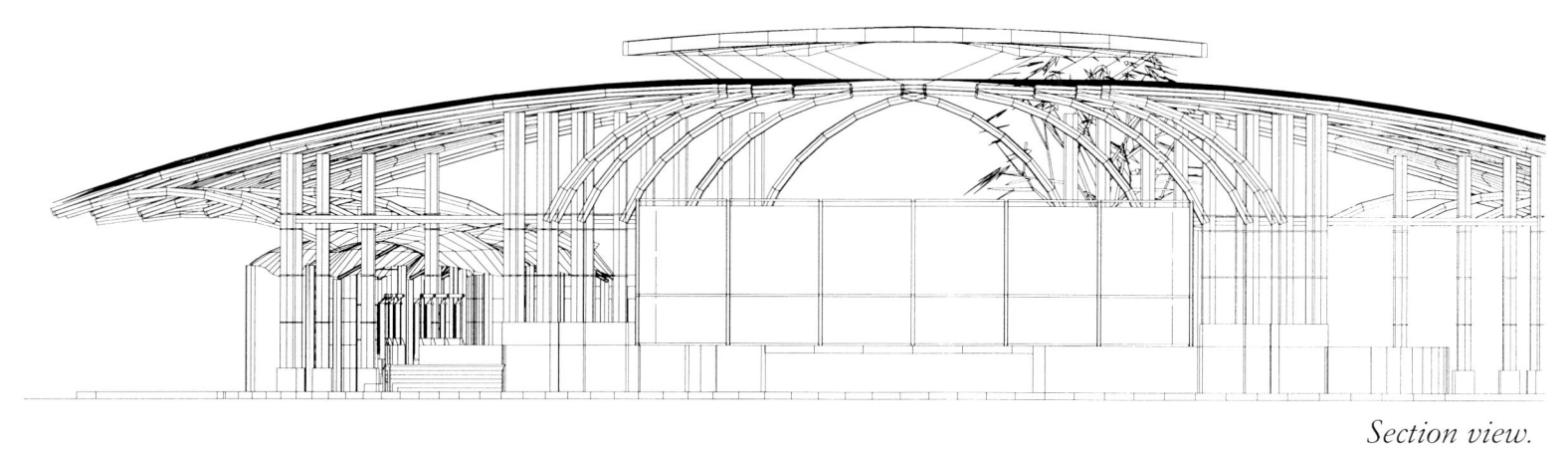

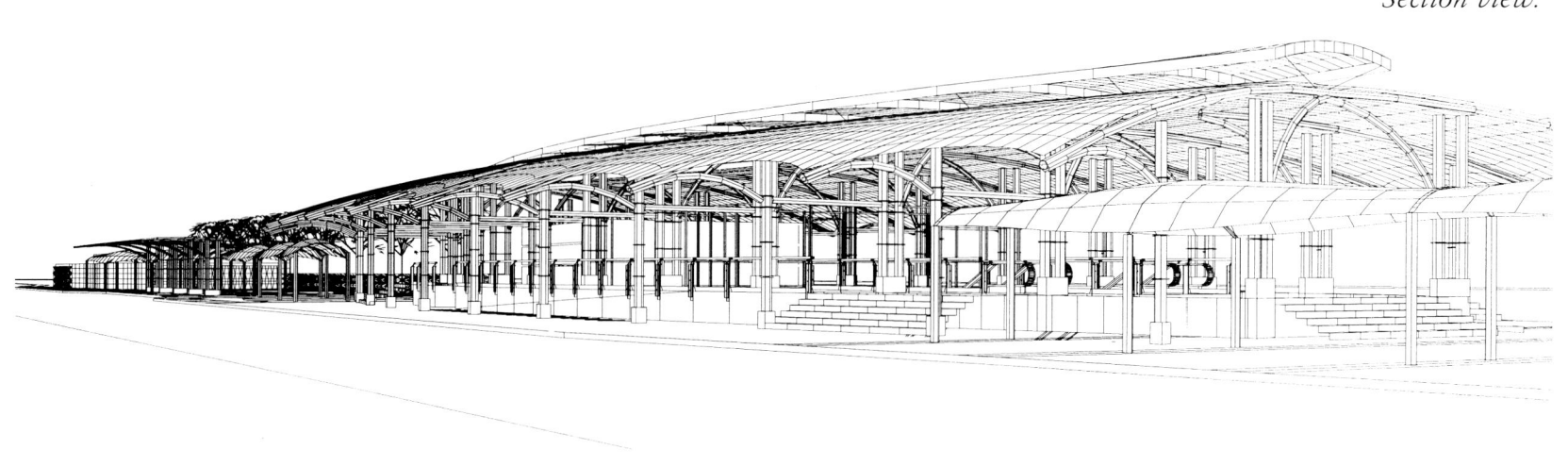

Section view.

Street view.

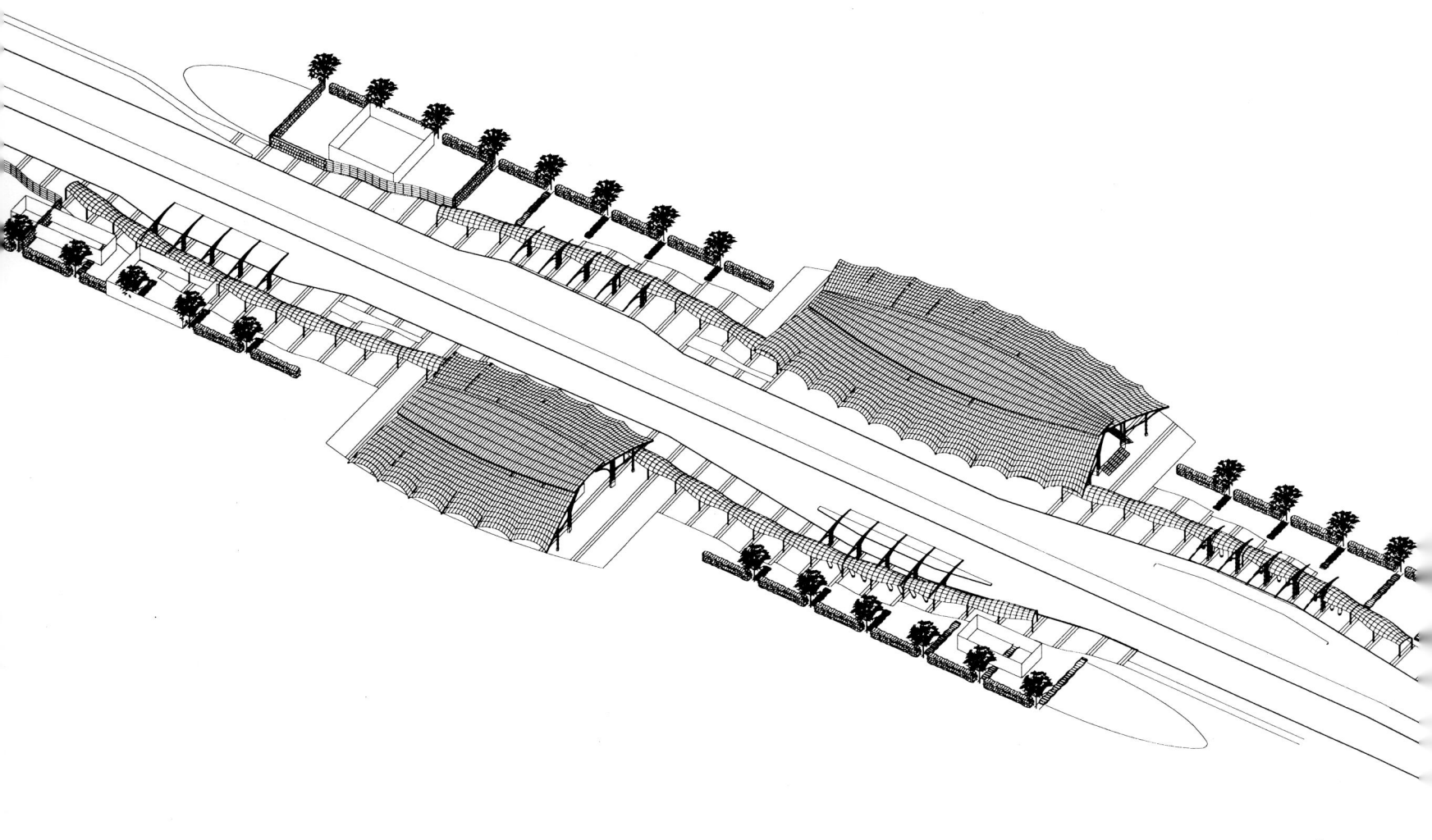

Axonometric view of site.

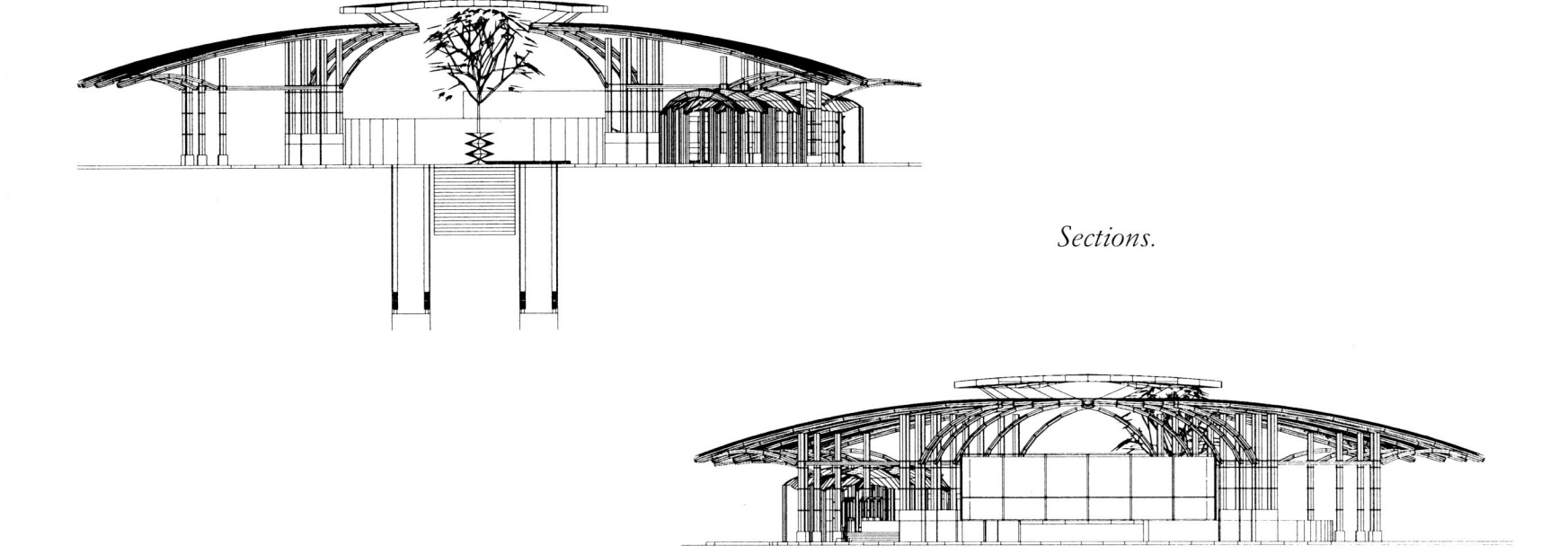

Sections.

View of fare gates.

View from mezzanine to platform.

View of mezzanine.

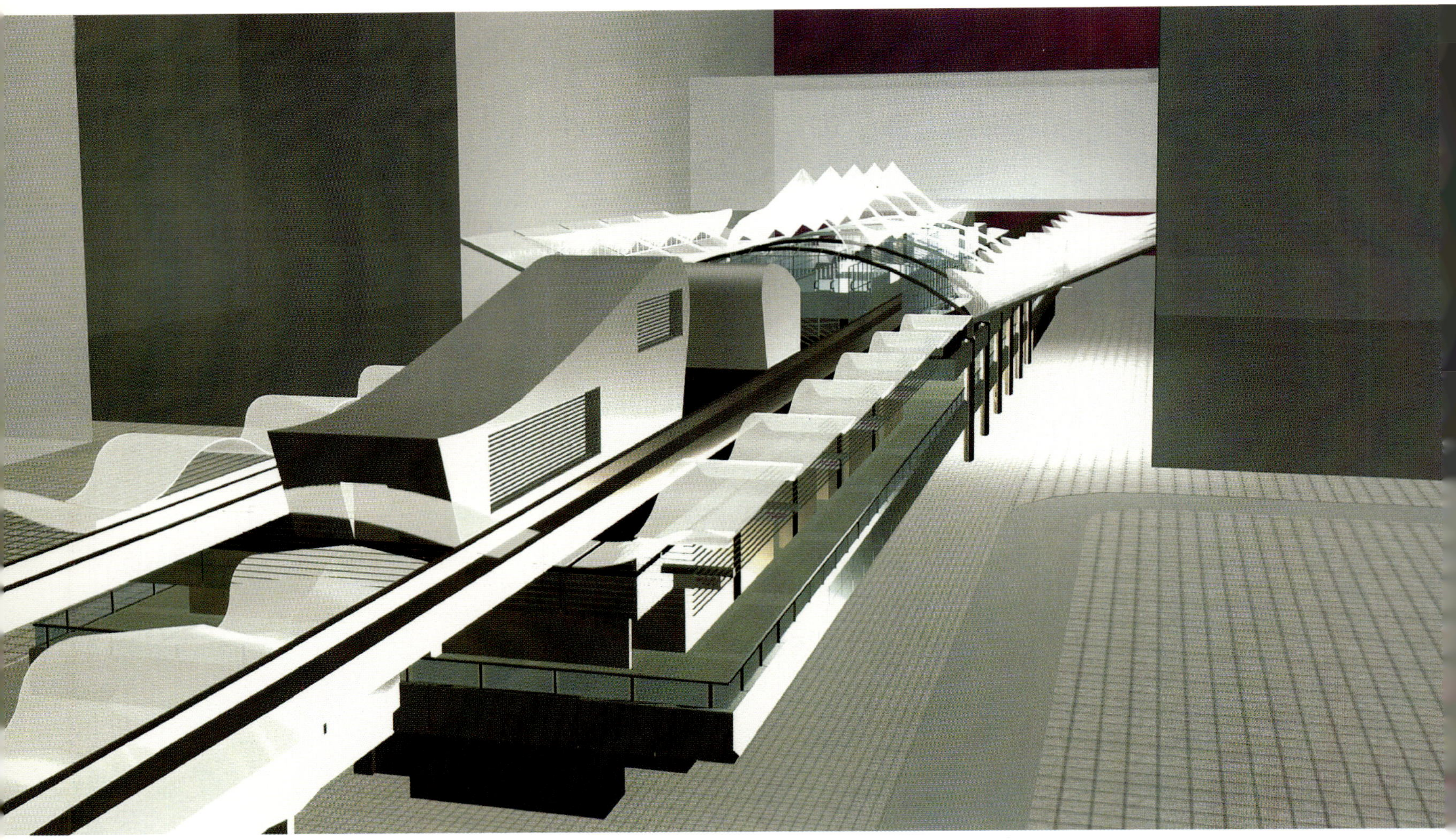

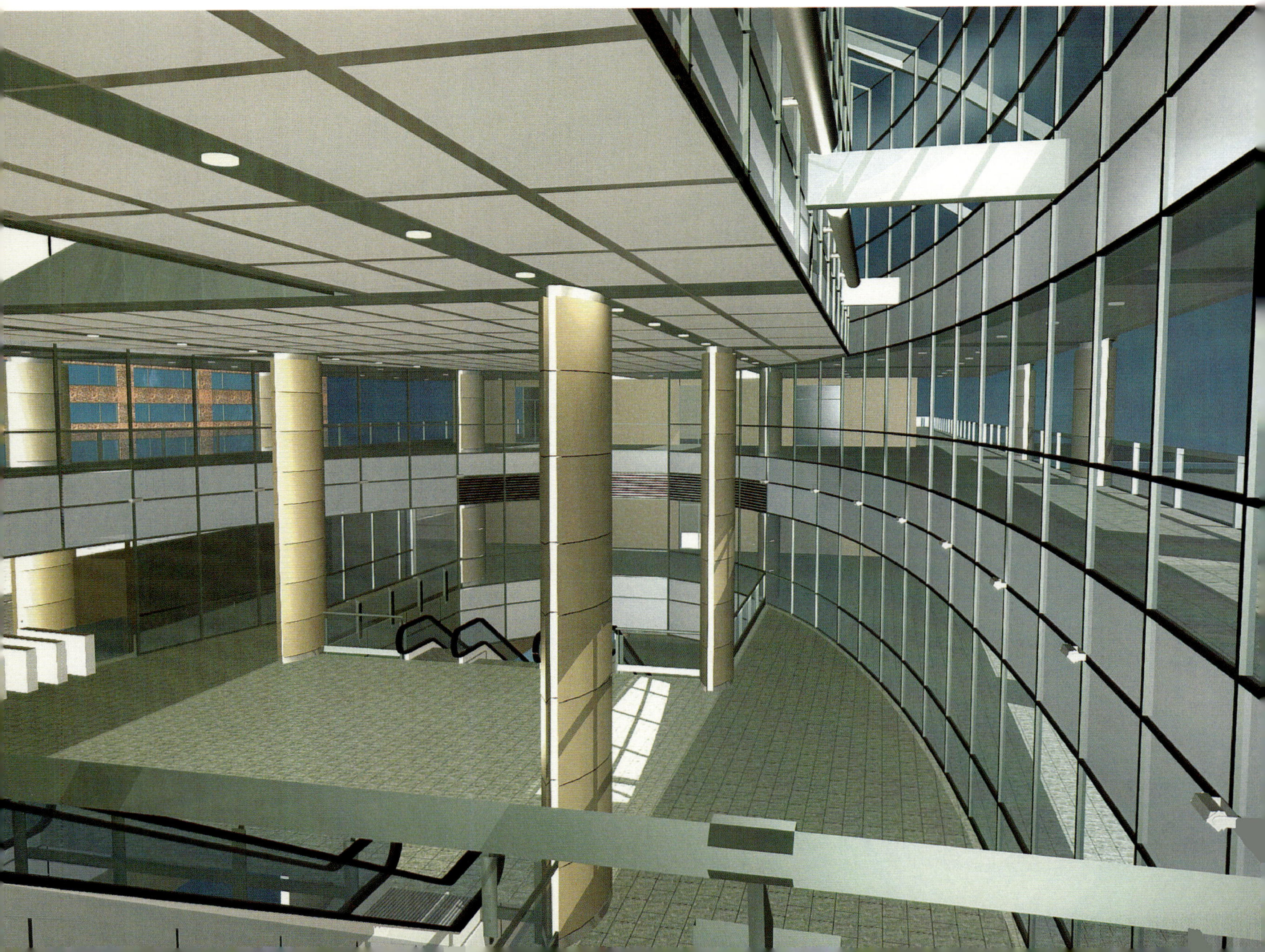

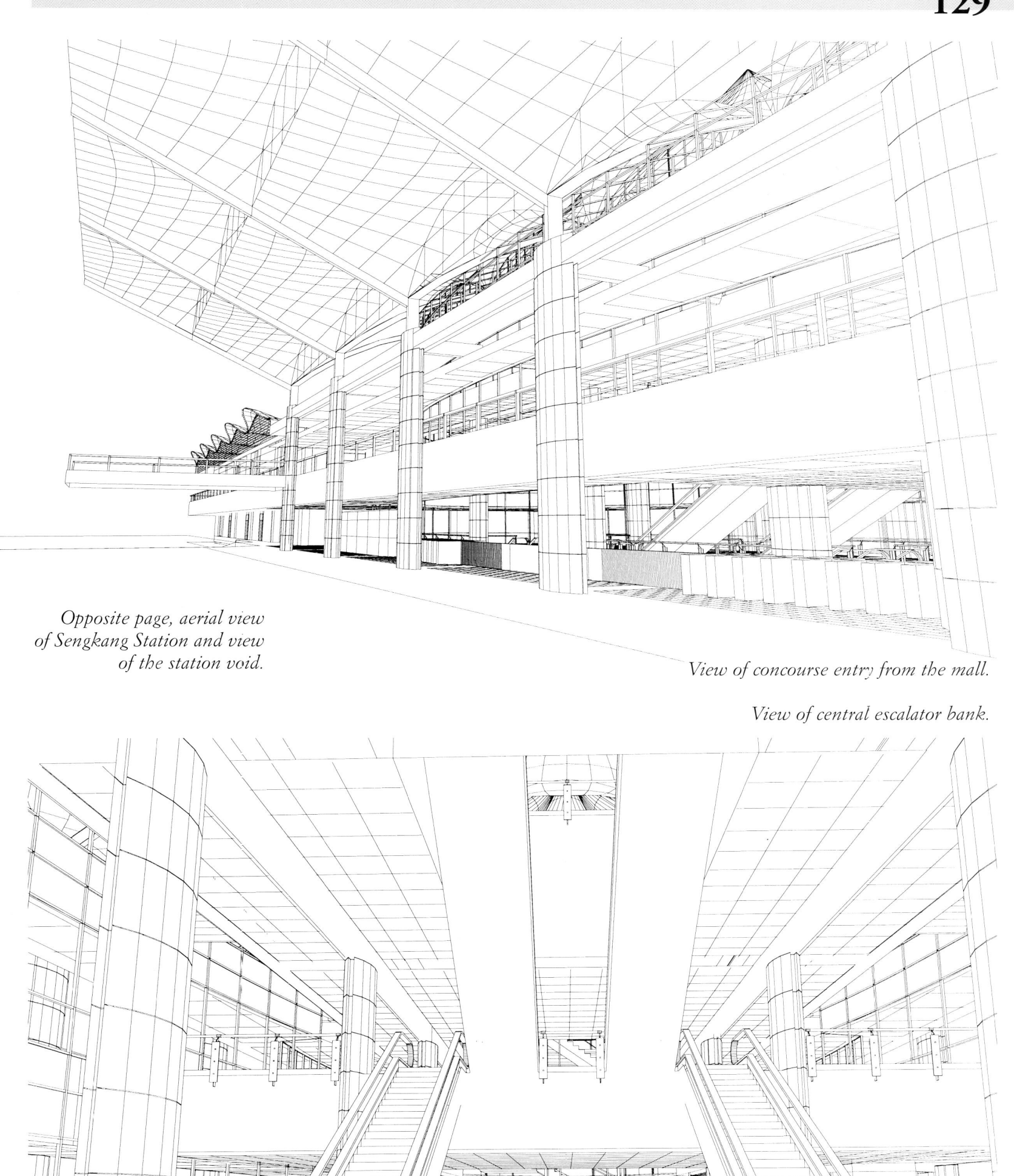

Opposite page, aerial view of Sengkang Station and view of the station void.

View of concourse entry from the mall.

View of central escalator bank.

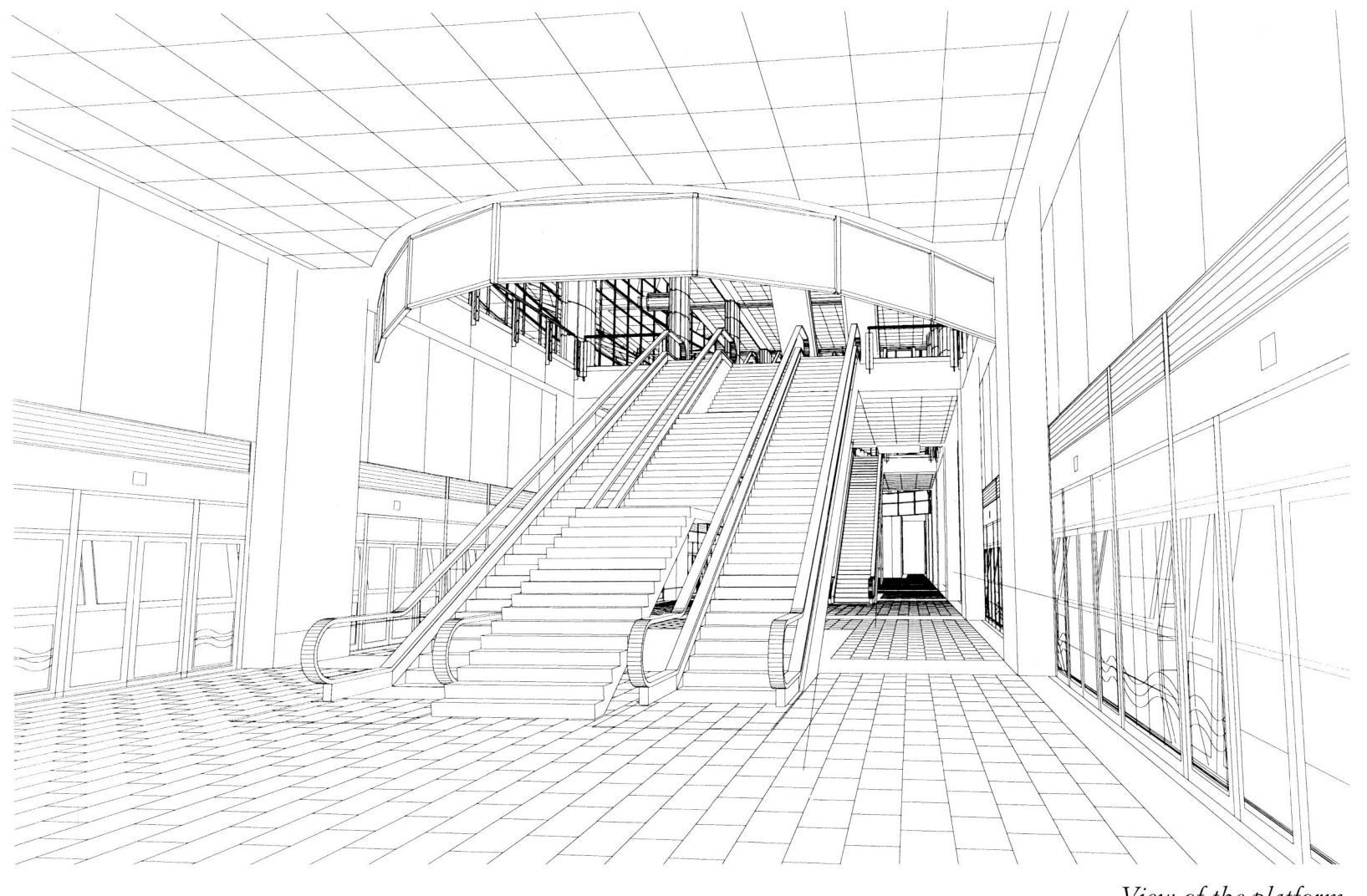

View of the platform.

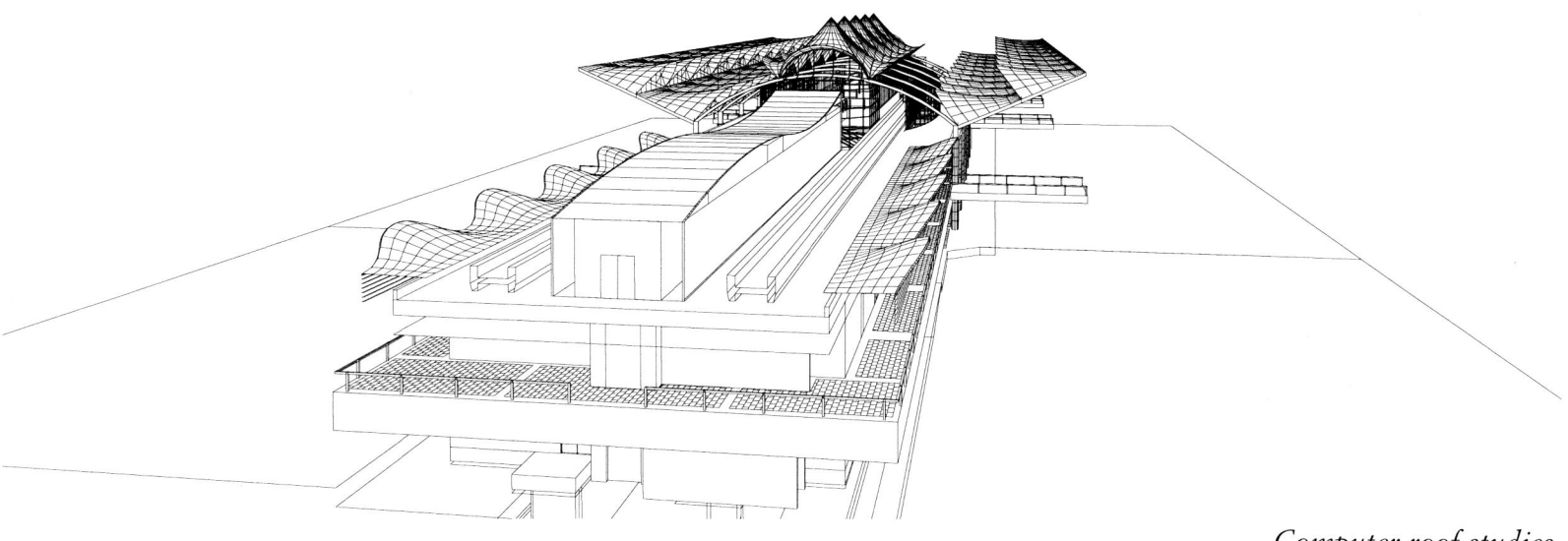

Computer roof studies.

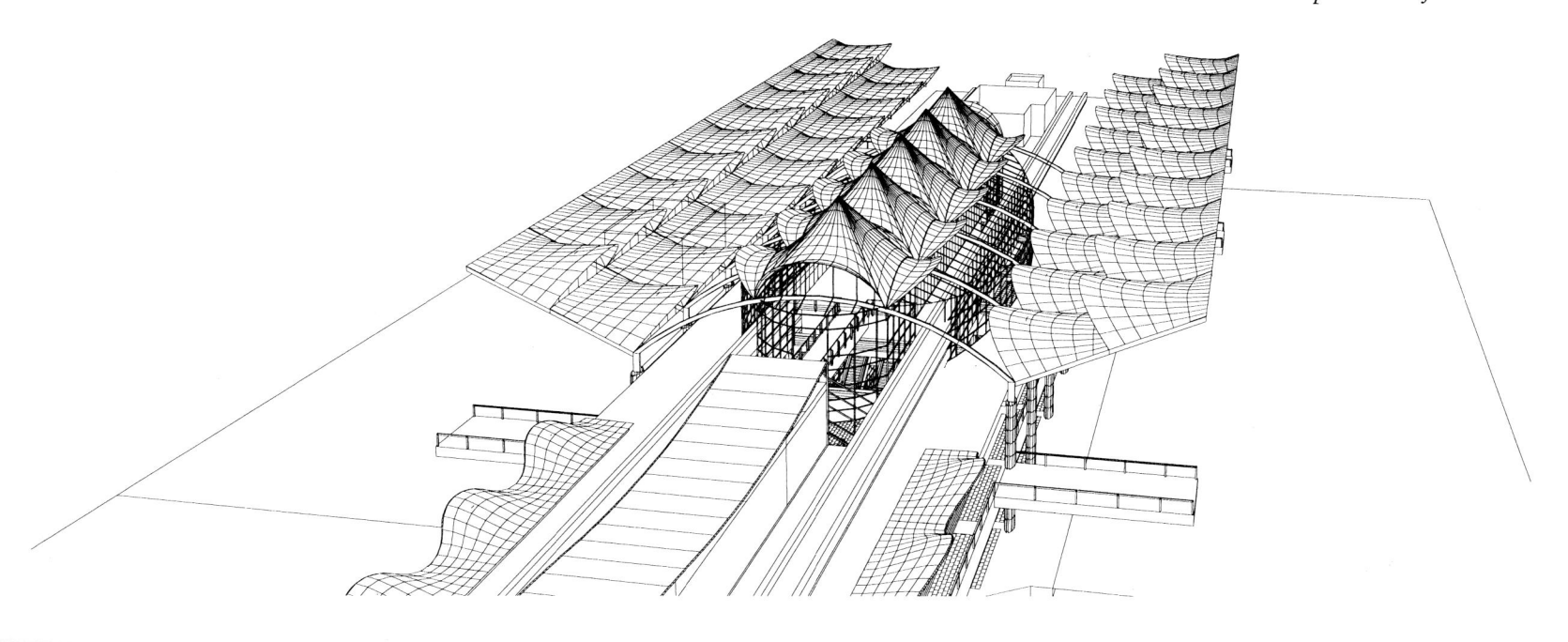

View of light rail platform.

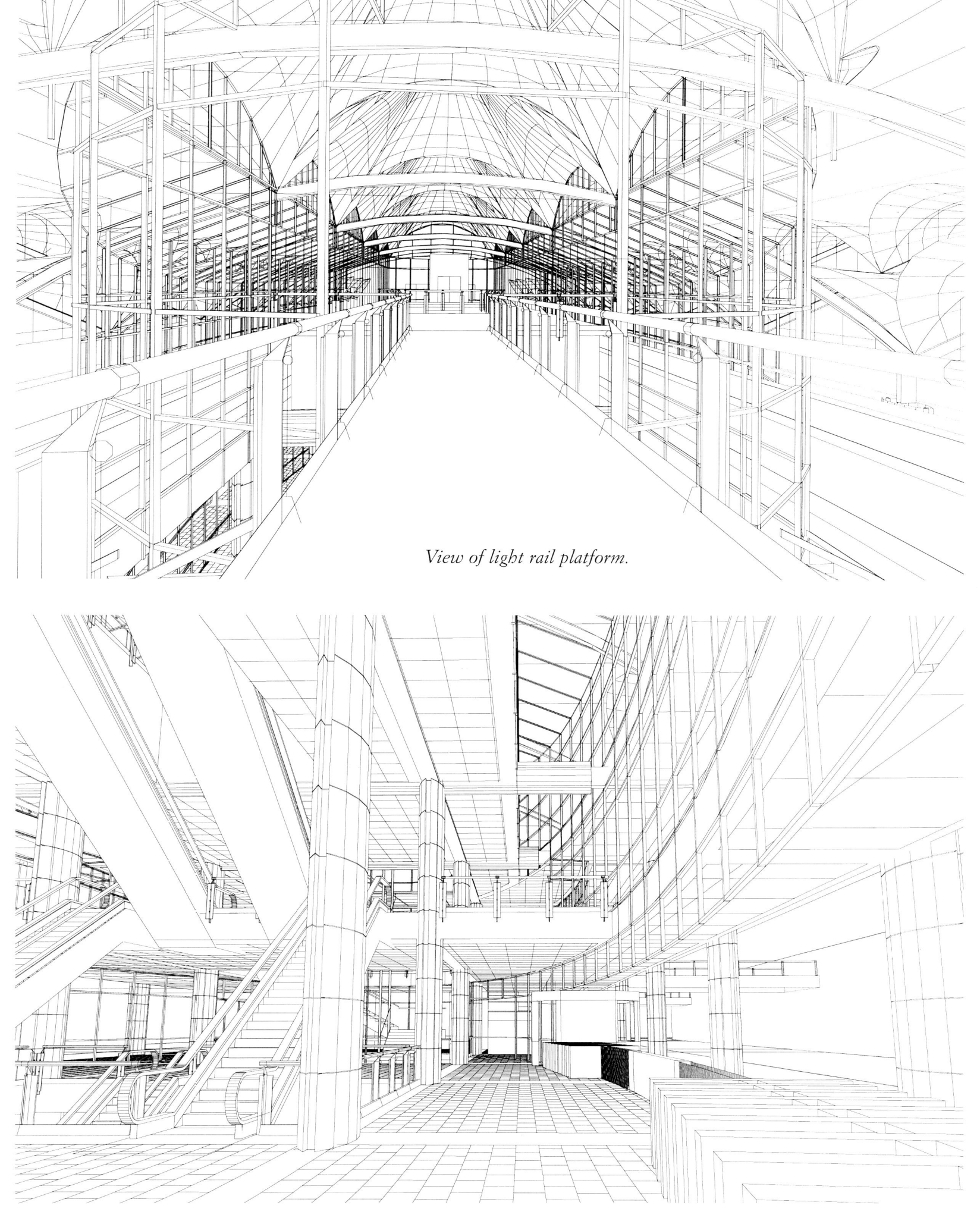

View of concourse fare gates.

132

View from platform up.

Mezzanine fare gates.

Mezzanine walkway.

Concourse fare gates.

Concourse fare gates.

Central escalator bank.

Views of the station void.

134

Dragon Tower

Symbolic in concept, the design of this 101-story superstructure reflects the strong national spirit that was emerging in Indonesia in the mid-1990s. Commissioned by the first lady of Indonesia and her advisors, the mixed-use tower is an icon of the nation's progress and of the collective optimism of the entire region.

In a gesture that reinforces this spirit, the architects at Altoon + Porter borrowed the concept of Pancasila – the five principles of the state philosophy – to form the base of the superstructure. The five pillars represent these ideals: the belief in one supreme God, justice and civility among peoples, the unity of Indonesia, democracy, and social justice. They became the foundation of the project. Four pillars anchor the corners of the tower, giving the form physical strength and visual lightness and drawing the eye immediately to the top of the fifth and highest pillar which completes the metaphorical depiction. Much like imagery evoked by the Statue of Liberty as she braces her weight against her stronghold foot and lifts her torch high, the form of Dragon Tower is braced securely and courageously against the natural elements.

Indonesia's indigenous architecture influenced the design for Dragon Tower. The diagonal bracing over the building's modern skin is an abstraction of the ubiquitous local textile, tapis. Used as a defense against the harsh Indonesian climate, the fabric is representative of a common method for seeking shelter used by a diverse population. This diagonal bracing also fortifies the structure, signifying the binding power of a common national purpose among a collage of races. The stepped faces of the structure are triangulated and terraced, drawing inspiration from the terraced buildings of Borobodur, the ancient Javanese worship site.

A series of atriums deliver light and air and allow the tower to soar in dramatic and unconventional ways. They also serve to unify the building with a strong vertical organization. The elevator cores are located on the façade, where they are drenched in daylight. Using advanced structural technology, half the building is braced horizontally from below at the transfer floors, while the other half rests securely on these bridge-like structures.

The interior of the project opens to a series of stacked, 24-story atriums that carry the building's express elevators to the uppermost levels. Played out on each of the three transfer floors of the express elevators are dining, conferencing, and other features that distribute energy and activity throughout the building.

Even the curved skin of Dragon Tower is reflective – both literally and figuratively. The timeless Indonesian sky is mirrored in the glazing that is part of the contemporary design and construction technologies used to create this national landmark.

View from east. *Theater view.*

View from west.

View from rear.

List of Works

1984

4000 WISCONSIN AVENUE
Office Building
Washington, DC

THE GRANDWAY
(Consulting Architects & Owner's Representative)
Multi-use Center
El Segundo, CA

1985

ENGINE COMPANY NO. 28
Adaptive Re-use
and Historic Preservation
Los Angeles, CA

BIGHORN INSTITUTE
Research Lab/Museum
Palm Desert, CA

THE CROSSROADS
Retail Center
Irvine, CA

3275 WILSHIRE
Architect's Office/Interior Architecture
Los Angeles, CA

FORT WORTH TOWN CENTER
Retail Center Renovation and Expansion
Fort Worth, TX

1986

NEWPORT HARBOR ART MUSEUM
Art Museum/Feasibility Study
Newport Beach, CA

ARDEN FAIR
Regional Retail Center
Sacramento, CA

MARINA MARKETPLACE
Retail Center
Marina del Rey, CA

REDMOND TOWN CENTER
Mixed-use Development
Redmond, WA

1987

THE GRAND AVENUE
Office Building/Historic Preservation
Los Angeles, CA

TRIANGLE SQUARE
Specialty/Entertainment
Retail Center
Costa Mesa, CA

LINCOLNWOOD TOWN CENTER
Regional Retail Center
Lincolnwood, IL

1988

ONE WILSHIRE BUILDING
Office/Interior Architecture/Renovation/Historic Preservation
Los Angeles, CA

TOWER PLACE
Urban Retail Center
Cincinnati, OH

CAREW TOWER
Renovation/Urban Retail Center/Historic Preservation
Cincinnati, OH

THE MALL AT GREEN HILLS
Regional Retail Center
Renovation/Expansion
Nashville, TN

1989

FASHION VALLEY CENTER
Regional Retail Center
Renovation/Expansion
San Diego, CA

FELIPE DE NEVE BRANCH LIBRARY
Library Renovation and Addition/Historic Preservation/Seismic Up-grade
Los Angeles, California

1990

SEVEN BRIDGES
Master Planning/Mixed-use Development
Chicago, IL

KAAHUMANU CENTER
Regional Retail/Entertainment Center
Renovation/Expansion
Kahului, Hawaii

5700 WILSHIRE
Architect's Office/Interior Architecture/Space Planning
Los Angeles, CA

1991

MULTI-USE DEVELOPMENT
Competition
Orlando, FL

KALEIDOSCOPE
Master Planning/Specialty/Entertainment
Retail Center
Mission Viejo, CA

SHERMAN OAKS GALLERIA
Urban Retail Center Renovation
Sherman Oaks, CA

LA JOLLA VILLAGE SQUARE
Regional Power Center
La Jolla, CA

1992

PACIFIC FINANCIAL PLAZA
Office/Mixed-use Renovation
Newport Beach, CA

SOUTHWESTERN UNIVERSITY
SCHOOL OF LAW
Space Planning/Interior Architecture
Los Angeles, CA

RANCHO SANTA MARGARITA
CITY CENTER
Master Planning/Retail Center
Rancho Santa Margarita, CA

SIQUEIROS MURAL
SHADE STRUCTURE
Shade Structure and Viewing Platform/Historic Preservation
Los Angeles, CA

NFL – YOUTH EDUCATION
TRAINING CENTER
Youth Learning/Athletic Center
Compton, CA

ECHO/HORIZON SCHOOL
Institutional/Renovation and Expansion/Historic Preservation
Culver City, CA

UCLA WOODEN CENTER EAST
Institutional/Office Building
Los Angeles, CA

1993

JAKARTA HOTEL
AND SHOPPING CENTER
Planning/Mixed-use Development
Jakarta, Indonesia

MCA UNIVERSAL STUDIOS
HOLLWOOD – EMPLOYEE SERVICES
COMPLEX
Office/Space Planning/Interiors
Universal City, CA

PICO/SAN VICENTE
Joint Development Study
for Metro Transit Station
Los Angeles, CA

BIGHORN INSTITUTE – RESIDENCE
Biologist Residence
Palm Desert, CA

1994

ALDERWOOD MALL
Regional Retail Center Renovation
Lynnwood, WA

THE GARDENS ON EL PASEO
Specialty Retail/Entertainment Galleria
Palm Desert, CA

VALENCIA TOWN CENTER
Retail/Entertainment Center
Renovation/Expansion
Valencia, CA

1995

UCLA JOHN WOODEN CENTER
EXPANSION
Institutional-Men's Gym/Dance/
Fitness/Armed Services ROTC/
classrooms/offices
Los Angeles, CA

WARRINGAH MALL STAGE I
Regional Retail Center Expansion
Sydney, Australia

1996

MARINA SQUARE
Regional Retail Center Renovation
Singapore

UCLA PARKING STRUCTURE #3
Parking Structure Expansion
Los Angeles, CA

KOTA BNI TRAIN STATION
Transit Station
Jakarta, Indonesia

MISSION VIEJO MALL
Regional Retail Center
Renovation/Expansion
Mission Viejo, CA

1997

DENVER WEST
Master Planning Specialty/Entertainment
Retail Center
Denver, CO

KINGDOM CENTRE
Mixed-use Development/Retail Center
Riyadh, Saudi Arabia

LOS ARCOS
Mixed-use Development
Phoenix, AZ

VALENCIA OFFICE/RETAIL
Office Building/Retail
Valencia, CA

BUANGKOK & SENGKANG
TRANSIT STATIONS
Transit Stations
Singapore

TAO YUAN CENTRE
Regional Retail Center
Taipei, Taiwan

KOWLOON STATION
Mixed-use Development/Retail
Hong Kong, China

KURSKY SQUARE
Retail Center
Moscow, Russia

WARRINGAH MALL STAGE II
Regional Retail Center Expansion
Sydney, Australia

SHAIKH ZAYED ROAD
Mixed-use Development
Dubai, Untied Arab Emirates

AL MAKTOUN
Mixed-use Development
Dubai, United Arab Emirates

Credits

4000 WISCONSIN AVENUE
Associate Architect
Stinson-Capelli Architects
Structural Engineer
Martin, Cagley and Associates
Mechanical / Electrical Engineer
Shefferman & Bibelson Company
Civil Engineer
Kidde Consultants
Geotechnical Engineer
Schnael Engineering Associates
Elevator Consulting Engineer
Lerch, Bates & Associates, Inc.
Fire Protection Engineer
Schirmer Engineering Corporation
Landscape Architect
Emmet L. Wemple & Associates
Lighting Designer
Theo Kondos, Inc.
Acoustical Engineer
Polysonics
Contractor
The Donohoe Construction Company, Inc.

ARDEN FAIR MALL
Structural Engineer
Robert Englekirk Structural Engineers, Inc.
Mechanical Engineer
Double O Engineering
Electrical Engineer
Store Matakovich & Wolfberg
Civil Engineer
CH2M Hill
Landscape Architect
Lawrence Reed Moline
Code / Fire Protection Consultant
Rolf Jensen & Associates, Inc.
Contractor
HCB Contractors

LINCOLNWOOD TOWN CENTER
Associate Architect
Christopher Rudolph, AIA
Structural Engineer
Tylk, Wright and Gustafson, Inc.
Mechanical Engineer
Dolio and Metz, Ltd.
Electrical / Plumbing Engineer
Technological Engineers, Inc.
Civil Engineer
Joseph A. Schudt & Associates
Code Consultant Engineer
Rolf Jenson Associates, Inc.
Landscape Architect
Lawrence Reed Moline, Ltd.
Lighting Designer
Theo Kondos, Inc.
Contractor
Inland Construction Co.

THE MALL AT GREEN HILLS
Structural Engineer
Stanley D. Lindsey and Associates, Ltd.
Mechanical Engineer
Double O Engineering, Inc.
Electrical Engineer
Store Matakovich & Wolfberg
Civil Engineer
Barge Waggoner, Sumner and Cannon
Soils Engineer
Engineering, Design & Geosciences Group, Inc.
Landscape Architect
Roy Ashley & Associates
Building Code / Fire Protection Engineer
Rolf Jensen & Associates, Inc.
Parking Design
International Parking Design, Inc.
Lighting Designer
Wheel Gersztoff Friedman Shankar, Inc.
Construction Specifier
Ralph Mellman & Associates
Contractor
McDevitt & Street Co.

TOWER PLACE
Associate Architect (Technical)
The FWA Group
Structural Engineer
King/Guinn Associates
Mechanical Engineer
Benner & Fields
Electrical Engineer
Engineers, Inc.
Traffic Engineer
Wilbur Smith & Associates
Life Safety / Building Code Engineer
Rolf Jensen & Associates, Inc.
Lighting Designer
Francis Krahe & Associates
Contractor
Turner Construction

KAAHUMANU CENTER
Structural Engineers
Robert Englekirk, Inc.
Mechanical Engineer / Subcontractor
Critchfield Mechanical, Inc.
Electrical Engineer
Moss Engineering
Civil Engineer
Ronald M. Fukumoto Enginerring, Inc.
Soils Engineer
Dames & Moore
Traffic Engineer
Austin, Tsutsumi & Associates, Inc.
Cinema Architect Consultant
Eugene E. Leucht Architects, LTD.
Code Consultant Engineer
Rolf Jensen & Associates, Inc.

Landscape Architect
Tongg Clarke & McCelvey
Lighting Designer
Wheel Gersztoff Friedman Shankar, Inc.
Specifications
Ralph Mellman & Associates
Fabric Roof
Birdair, Inc.
Construction Manager
KX Corporation
Contractor
Keller Construction/U.S.P.B.

FASHION VALLEY CENTER
Structural Engineer
Robert Englekirk, Inc.
Electrical Engineer
Nikolakopulos & Associates
Plumbing Engineer
Store Matakovich & Wolfberg
Civil Engineer
Rick Engineering
Soils Engineer
Woodward-Clyde Consultant
Fire Protection / Building Code Consultant Engineer
Rolf Jensen & Associates, Inc.
Traffic Circulation Engineer
Linscott, Law & Greenspan Engineer
Traffic Engineer
Urban Systems Associates, Inc.
Landscape Architect
Wimmer Yamada Associates
Lighting Designer
Francis Krahe & Associates
Specifications
Ralph Mellman & Associates
Parking Consultant
Walker Parking Consultants/Engineers, Inc.
Cost Estimator
Campbell-Anderson & Associates, Inc.
Contractor
Robert E. Bayley Construction

THE GARDENS ON EL PASEO
Structural Engineer
Brandow and Johnston Associates
Mechanical / Plumbing Engineer
Store Matakovich & Wolfberg
Electrical Engineer
Nikolakopulos & Associates
Civil Engineer
ASL Consulting Engineers
Code / Fire Protection Consultant Engineers
Rolf Jensen and Associates, Inc.
Landscape Architect
Design Workshop
Specifications

Ralph Mellman and Associates
Specialty Lighting Designer
Patrick Quigley and Associates
Traffic / Parking
Linscott, Law & Greenspan
Parking Consultant
Walker Parking Consultants
Geology & Soils Engineers
Earth Systems Consultants
Contractor
Snyder Landston Real Estate & Services

BIGHORN INSTITUTE RESIDENCE
Structural Engineer
David D.B. Johnson Structural Engineer
Mechanical Engineer
Double O Engineering
Electrical Engineer
Nikolakopulos & Associates
Civil Engineer
ASL Consulting Engineers
Construction / Specification
Ralph P. Mellman & Associates
Soil Engineer
Earth Systems Consultants
Contractor
Lyle Parks Jr. General Contractor

SHADE STRUCTURE
FOR THE SIQUIEROS MURAL
Structural Engineer
Structure Technology, Inc.
Code Consultant
Rolf Jensen & Associates, Inc.

ECHO / HORIZON SCHOOL
Structural Engineer
Johnson & Nielsen Associates
Mechanical Engineer
Double O Engineering
Electrical Engineer
Nikolakopulos & Associates
Landscape Architect
Melendrez & Associates
Civil Engineer
Mollenhauer, Higashi & Moore, Inc.
Soils Engineer
Geotechnical Professional, Inc.
Contractor
Del Amo Construction, Inc.

MCA-USH EMPLOYEE
SERVICES COMPLEX
Structural Engineer
David D.B. Johnson
Mechanical Engineer
Store Matakovich & Wolfberg
Electrical Engineer
Nikolakopulos & Associates
Acoustical Consultant
Marshall Long Acoustics
Code Consultant
Rolf Jensen & Associates, Inc.
Fixture, Furniture & Equipment
Freeman Designs
Cost Estimator
William F. Mullen
Contractor
Ray Wilson Company

SOUTHWESTERN UNIVERSITY
SCHOOL OF LAW LIBRARY
Structural Engineer
Englekirk & Sabol Consulting
Engineers, Inc.
Mechanical / Electrical / Pluming Engineer

Store Matakovich & Wolberg
Civil Engineer
Mollenhauer, Higashi & Moore, Inc.
Fire Protection / Code Consultant
Rolf Jensen & Associates, Inc.
Program Management
Peck / Jones
Interiors Consultant
Freeman Designs
Lighting Designer
WGSS
Specifications
Ralph P. Mellman Associates
Contractor
Pueblo Contracting Services

UCLA WOODEN EAST BUILDNG
Structural Engineer
Brandow & Johnston
Mechanical / Electrical / Plumbing Engineer
Store Matakovich & Wolfberg
Civil Engineer
RBA Partners, Inc.
Specification Writer
CMS Consultant

UCLA PARKING STRUCTURE #3
EXPANSION
Structural Engineer
Englekirk & Sabol
Mechanical / Electrical / Plumbing
Store Matakovich & Wolfberg
Civil Engineer
RBA Partner, Inc.
Landscape Architects
LRM, Ltd.
Contractor
Ray Wilson Co.

TAMAN ANGGREK
SHOPPING CENTER
AND CONDOMINIUM
Associate Architect
Heah Hock Heng & Partners
Structural Engineer
Martin, Middlebrook & Louie
Mechanical / Electrical Engineer
PCR Engineers Pte Ltd
Code / Fire Protection
Rolf Jensen & Associates, Inc.
Parking Consultant
Kaku Associates
Landscape Architect
Emmet L. Wemple & Associates
Lighting Designer
Theo Kondos Associates, Inc.
Ice Skating Rink Consultant
Paul J. Ruffing, AIA
Fountain / Water Feature
Aquatic Design Group
Graphic Designer
David Carter Design Associates
Architectural Illustrator
Barry Zauss Associates
Architectural Illustrator
Robert De Rosa
Architectural Illustrator
Jon Messer
Architectural Illustrator
David A. Suplee

JAKARTA HOTEL AND
SHOPPING CENTER
Interior Designer
Hirsch Bedner Associates
Parking Consultant

Kaku Associates Corporation
Landscape Architects
Emmet L. Wemple & Associates
Architectural Illustrator
Barry Zauss Associates
Architectural Illustrator
Robert De Rosa
Glendale, CA

WARRINGAH MALL
Associate Architect
Thrum Architects Pty Limited
Structural Engineer
Hyder Consulting Australia Pty Ltd
Electrical Engineer / Lighting Designer
Barry Webb & Associates (NSW) Pty Ltd
Code Consultant
Scientific Services Laboratory
Interior Design
MBBD
Landscape Architect
Site Image
Quantity Surveyor
Rider Hunt
Fabric Roof
Birdair, Inc.
SpaceTech
Operations
Resolve Engineering

MRT 702 STATIONS
SENKANG / BUANGKOK STATIONS
Associate Architect
Heah Hock Heng & Partners
Lighting Consultant
Francis Krahe & Associates, Inc.

ALTOON + PORTER Architects
Staff 1984-1998

The projects shown in this volume represent the work of the following individuals.
We have made every effort to ensure that the names and dates are complete and correct but we apologize for any errors or omissions.

1984

Ronald A. Altoon
James F. Porter
Harvey R. Niskala

Jack Fong
Susan Ford

1985

Ronald A. Altoon
James F. Porter
Harvey R. Niskala

Evelyn Abramson
Maryati Benniardi
Gary Dempster
Jack Fong
Susan Ford
Hendra Kusuma
Daniel Kwok
Julie Lamprecht
William Sebring
Marilyn Wong

1986

Ronald A. Altoon
James F. Porter
Harvey R. Niskala

Evelyn Abramson
Jason Balinbin
Thomas Bastis
Rafael Caballero
Dan Cockrell
Gary Dempster
Leslie Fernald
Jack Fong
Susan Ford
Marvin Ginsberg
James Hansen
Tracey Hardwick
Hans Herst
William Huang
Maryati Imanto
C. Karung
Jeanne Kinney
Hendra Kusuma
Daniel Kwok
Julie Lamprecht
Randolph Larsen
Rny Madale
Klayden Malekpourani
Carl Meyer
John Oda
Damon Porter
Jerome Radin
Karen Safer
James Salazar
Jeffrey Schneider
Linda Scott
William Sebring
Anne Trelease
Glenn Williams
Marilyn Wong
Bill Yee
Chien Yeh
Michael Zakian

1987

Ronald A. Altoon
James F. Porter
Harvey R. Niskala

Evelyn Abramson
Bryoe Ambrazienas
Jason Balinbin
Rafael Caballero
Dan Cockrell
Rollie Cruz
Gary Dempster
Leslie Fernald
Jack Fong
Susan Ford
Marvin Ginsberg
James Hansen
Tracey Hardwick
Hans Herst
Maryati Imanto
Stephen Ip
Jeanne Kinney
Mary Kopitzke
Hendra Kusuma
Daniel Kwok
Julie Lamprecht
Randolph Larsen
Nancy Long
Rny Madale
Kenneth McKently
Carl Meyer
John Oda
Arran Porter
Jerome Radin
Karen Safer
James Salazar
Jeffrey Schneider
Margaret Schwartz
Linda Scott
William Sebring
Fay Sveltz
Anne Trelease
Glenn Williams
Marilyn Wong
Bill Yee
Chien Yeh
Michael Zakian

1988

Ronald A. Altoon
James F. Porter
Harvey R. Niskala

Troy Auzenne
JoDee Becker
Rafael Caballero
Dan Cockrell
Rollie Cruz
Michael Delaney
Gary Dempster
Jack Fong
Susan Ford
Aida Gabaldon
Marvin Ginsberg
Barrington Gowdy
James Hansen
Tracey Hardwick
Hans Herst
Matthew Imadomi
Maryati Imanto
Stephen Ip
Peter Jung
Jeanne Kinney
Mary Kopitzke
Hendra Kusuma
Daniel Kwok
Julie Lamprecht
Randolph Larsen
Manki Lee
Kenneth Long
Carl Meyer
Fred Meyer
Ellen Miller
Alleta Nesbit
Benjamin Oyeka
Jane Paget
Ellen Pollard
A. Racho
Edward Robison
Francine Sacco
Karen Safer
James Salazar
Margaret Schwartz
Linda Scott
William Sebring
JoAnn Sheu
Marta Recio Slagter
Ruben Torres
Anne Trelease
Eva Waters
Marilyn Wong
Nushin Yazdi
Chien Yeh
Michael Zakian

1989

Ronald A. Altoon
James F. Porter
Harvey R. Niskala

Leticia Aclan
Eric Altoon
Vaughn Babcock
Gaila Barnett
JoDee Becker
Ronald Benson
Tina Bernardo
Ellen Cabrerra
Ruben Catabas
Jin Chun
Rollie Cruz
Michael Delaney
Gary Dempster
Adriana Donea
Hillary Fleischer
Jack Fong
Cindy Fox
Marvin Ginsberg
Erwin Gomez
Hector Gomez
James Hansen
Hans Herst
Shannon Holderman
Maryati Imanto
Matthew Inadomi
Peter Jung
Mary Kopitzke
Gary Krenz
Hendra Kusuma
Julie Lamprecht
Randolph Larsen
Manki Lee
I-Joen Lin
Kenneth Long
Gaylord Melton
Carl Meyer
Fred Meyer
Ellen Miller
Alleta Nesbit
Benjamin Oyeka
Jane Paget
Angelito Pasamonte
Maria Quandt
Tom Robertson
Julie Robinson
Karen Safer
Margaret Schwartz
William Sebring
JoAnn Sheu
Marta Recio Slagter
Ruben Torres
Anne Trelease
Suzy Vernoff
Marilyn Wong
Annette Wu
Liming Yang
Nushin Yazdi

1990

Ronald A. Altoon
James F. Porter
Harvey R. Niskala
Gary K. Dempster
Carl F. Meyer

Leticia Aclan
Eric Altoon
James Auld
Vaughn Babcock
Gaila Barnett
JoDee Becker
Ronald Benson
Ellen Cabrerra
Ruben Catabas
Jin Chun
Michael Delaney
Adriana Donea
Hillary Fleischer
Jack Fong
Cindy Fox
Marvin Ginsberg
Erwin Gomex
Hector Gomez
David Greunke
James Hansen
Jane Hendricks
Shannon Holderman
Mariati Imanto
Peter Jung
Robin Kerper
Mary Kopitzke
Gary Krenz
Hendra Kusuma
Julie Lamprecht
Randolph Larsen
Manki Lee
Kenneth Long
Steven McEntee
Gaylord Melton
Fred Meyer
Ellen Miller
Benjamin Oyeka
Angelito Pasamonte
Jose Pimental
Maria Quandt
Tom Robertson
Julie Robinson
Karen Safer
Margaret Schwartz
William Sebring
Leonarda Seward
JoAnn Sheu
Marta Recio Slagter
Thai Ta
Ruben Torres
Suzy Vernoff
Marilyn Wong
Annette Wu
Liming Yang
Nushin Yazdi

1991

Ronald A. Altoon
James F. Porter
Harvey R. Niskala
Gary K. Dempster
Carl F. Meyer

Leticia Aclan
Dale Addy
James Auld
Gaila Barnett
Giovanni Bignasca
Ellen Cabrerra
Sandra Cervantes-Caraballo
Michael Delaney
Julie Flattery
Jack Fong
Cindy Fox
Hector Gomez
James Hansen
Shannon Holderman
Maryati Imanto
Mary Kopitzke
Gary Krenz
Hendra Kusuma
Kim Landau
Randolph Larsen
Kenneth Long

Steven McEntee
Fred Meyer
Ellen Miller
Karen Safer
Margaret Schwartz
William Sebring
Andrea Stein
Thai Ta
Suzy Vernoff
Annette Wu
Libing Yan

1992

Ronald A. Altoon
James F. Porter
Harvey R. Niskala
Gary K. Dempster
Carl F. Meyer

James Auld
Ronald Benson
Giovanni Bignasca
Ellen Cabrerra
Sandra Cervantes-
 Caraballo
Jin Chun
Ann Davidson
Jeff Fineman
Julie Flattery
Jack Fong
Cindy Fox
Hector Gomez
John Gormley
Eva Gryczon
James Hansen
Tiffany Hartley
Shannon Holderman
Ronald Hutchens
Maryati Imanto
Charles Johnson
Mohan Joshi
Gary Krenz
Hendra Kusuma
Kim Landau
Randolph Larsen
Fred Meyer
Ellen Miller
Lourdes Nishi
Cynthia Phakos
Margaret Schwartz
William Sebring
Thai Ta
Lisa Tucker
Libing Yan
Hraztan Zeitlian

1993

Ronald A. Altoon
James F. Porter
Harvey R. Niskala
Gary K. Dempster
Carl F. Meyer

James Auld
Kim Bedrosian
Ronald Benson
Sandra Cervantes-
 Caraballo
Jin Chun
E. Cialic
Ann Davidson
Jeff Fineman
Jack Fong
Cindy Fox
Hector Gomez
John Gormley
James Hansen
Tiffany Hartley
Shannon Holderman
Ronald Hutchens

Maryati Imanto
Charles Johnson
Louis Kaufman
Gary Krenz
Hendra Kusuma
Randolph Larsen
Carmel McFayden
Sabrina Medrano
Fred Meyer
Ellen Miller
Cindy Panameno
Cynthia Phakos
Margaret Schwartz
William Sebring
Mark Shaw
Thai Ta
Lisa Tucker
Libing Yan
Hraztan Zeitlian

1994

Ronald A. Altoon
James F. Porter
Harvey R. Niskala
Gary K. Dempster
Carl F. Meyer

Vivien Adao
James Auld
Darrell Bandur
Kim Bedrosian
Ronald Benson
Humberto Bermudez
Sandra Cervantes-
 Caraballo
Ian Cha
Donna Chinchar
Jin Chun
Ann Davidson
Delores Deck
Paul Enseki
Jeff Fineman
Jack Fong
Cindy Fox
Art Garcia
Hector Gomez
John Gormley
James Hansen
Philip Han
Antoine Harb
Shannon Holderman
Ronald Hutchens
Maryati Imanto
Charles Johnson
Mohan Joshi
Kevin Joyce
Louis Kaufman
Fred Kerz
Ann Knudsen
Gary Krenz
Pamela Ku
Hendra Kusuma
Randolph Larsen
Mitch Lawrence
Paul Li
Chen Lu
Frank Lu
Carmel McFayden
Sabrina Medrano
Angela Mercer
Fred Meyer
Ellen Miller
Cindy Ng
Cindy Panameno
Purnima Patil
Trevor Pollard
Mohan Pradhan
Evelyn Prinz
Ricardo Santia
Kristi Schneider
Margaret Schwartz
William Sebring

Mark Shaw
Andie Squires
Thai Ta
Lisa Tucker
Manuel Vargas
Huey Vuong
Sylvia Wallis
Evette Westbrook
Libing Yan
Hraztan Zeitlian

1995

Ronald A. Altoon
James F. Porter
Harvey R. Niskala
Gary K. Dempster
Carl F. Meyer

Vivien Adao
Ryan Altoon
James Auld
Theresa Baker
Darrell Bandur
Ronald Benson
Humberto Bermudez
Sandra Cervantes-
 Caraballo
Ian Cha
Jack Fong
Hector Gomez
John Gormley
Philip Han
Cindy Hoebink
Shannon Holderman
Ronald Hutchens
Charles Johnson
Kevin Joyce
Louis Kaufman
Fred Kerz
Ann Knudsen
Gary Krenz
Hendra Kusuma
Randolph Larsen
Mitch Lawrence
Paul Li
Kenneth Long
Carmel McFayden
Sabrina Medrano
Angela Mercer
Fred Meyer
Ellen Miller
Blythe Million
Cindy Ng
Michelle Niskala
Purnima Patil
Trevor Pollard
Mohan Pradhan
Evelyn Prinz
Margaret Schwartz
William Sebring
Mark Shaw
Art Simonian
Andie Squires
Thai Ta
Manuel Vargas
Sylvia Wallis
Hraztan Zeitlian

1996

Ronald A. Altoon
James F. Porter
Gary K. Dempster
Carl F. Meyer

Ryan Altoon
Stephen Andrews
James Auld
Theresa Baker
Ronald Benson
Humberto Bermudez

Sandra Cervantes-
 Caraballo
Ian Cha
Suzanne Dvells
Jack Fong
Hector Gomez
John Gormley
Kenneth Grobecker
Philip Han
Cindy Hoebink
Ronald Hutchens
Kevin Joyce
Louis Kaufman
Fred Kerz
Ann Knudsen
Gary Krenz
Hendra Kusuma
Randolph Larsen
Mitch Lawrence
Raymond Leung
Paul Li
Chin Lim
Kenneth Long
Carmel McFayden
Angela Mercer
Colette Meyer
Fred Meyer
Cindy Ng
Ung Ngu
Lisa Park
Trevor Pollard
Evelyn Prinz
Kate Russell
Tim Sakamoto
Margaret Schwartz
William Sebring
Mark Shaw
Art Simonian
Andie Squires
Thai Ta
Julia Tschiersch
Manuel Vargas
Sylvia Wallis
Julian Yip

1997

Ronald A. Altoon
James F. Porter
Gary K. Demspter
Carl F. Meyer

James Auld
Theresa Baker
Ronald Benson
Humberto Bermudez
DeeAnn Bollow
Sandra Cervantes-
 Caraballo
Ian Cha
Alison Covert
Moon-Song Empig
Jack Fong
Hector Gomez
John Gormley
Kenneth Grobecker
Philip Han
Ronald Hutchens
Kevin Joyce
Louis Kaufman
Fred Kerz
Ann Knudsen
Gary Krenz
Hendra Kusuma
Randolph Larsen
Mitch Lawrence
Raymond Leung
Paul Li
Chin Lim
Kenneth Long
Carmel McFayden
Angela Mercer
Carinne Meyer

Colette Meyer
Douglas Meyer
Fred Meyer
Hiroko Miyake
Matthew Nelson
Michael O'Sullivan
Mark Owen
Trevor Pollard
Beverly Powell
Evelyn Prinz
Brian Russell
Kate Russell
Yasuyuki Sakarai
Shahan Sanossian
Margaret Schwartz
William Sebring
Mark Shaw
Art Simonian
Andie Squires
Olesia Stefurak
Thai Ta
Manuel Vargas
Sylvia Wallis
Leslie Young

1998 (through April)

Ronald A. Altoon
James F. Porter
Gary K. Dempster
Carl F. Meyer

Paula Arviso
James Auld
Theresa Baker
Ronald Benson
Humberto Bermudez
DeeAnn Bollow
Sandra Cervantes-
 Caraballo
Margaret Cheung
Alison Covert
Moon-Song Empig
Jack Fong
John Gormley
David Green
Philip Han
Ronald Hutchens
Kevin Joyce
Louis Kaufman
Fred Kerz
Joshua Kimmel
Ann Knudsen
Gary Krenz
Hendra Kusuma
Randolph Larsen
Mitch Lawrence
Raymond Leung
Paul Li
Chin Lim
Fang Liu
Kenneth Long
Douglas Meyer
Fred Meyer
Hiroko Miyake
Matthew Nelson
Michael O'Sullivan
Mark Owen
Beverly Powell
Brian Russell
Kate Russell
Yasuyuki Sakarai
William Sebring
Mark Shaw
Art Simonian
Olesia Stefurak
Thai Ta
Kanit Tantiwong
Paul Tran
Manuel Vargas
Jon Vaszauskas
Sylvia Wallis
Leslie Young